Seasons
in
Spirituality

Robert P. Maloney, C.M.

Seasons in Spirituality

Reflections on Vincentian Spirituality in Today's World

New City Press

Published in the United States by New City Press
202 Cardinal Rd., Hyde Park, NY 12538
©1998 Robert P. Maloney, C. M.

Cover design by Nick Cianfarani

Library of Congress Cataloging-in-Publication Data:
A catalog record for this book is available from the Library of Congress

ISBN 1-56548-095-3

Printed in Canada

"Grace has its moments."

Vincent de Paul to Bernard Codoing
March 16, 1644

Contents

Preface

For centuries Vincent de Paul has attracted women and men of all social strata to join in the service of the poor. The reason is simple: He offers a practical spirituality that is extremely appealing. He urges us to love God "with the sweat of our brow and the strength of our arms" (SV XI, 40). But he is by no means an activist. In fact, those who knew this great saint of charity considered him a contemplative. He was convinced that someone who prays can do everything (SV XI, 83).

I write this book for all those who would like to know Vincent de Paul better. He is very lovable. I encourage you to let him speak to you with his characteristic directness. Listen to him attentively as he says: "There is no better way to assure our eternal happiness than to live and die in the service of the poor within the arms of providence and to deny ourselves by following Jesus Christ" (SV III, 392).

In a special way, I offer these essays to the millions of members of our rapidly growing Vincentian Family. In this past year I have spoken again and again, in different countries, to the numerous groups who live in Saint Vincent's spirit: the Congregation of the Mission, the Daughters of Charity, the International Association of Charities (the former "Ladies of Charity"), the Vincent de Paul Society, the Vincentian Marian Youth Groups, the Miraculous Medal Association, various communities of Sisters of Charity, and many other associations that have Saint Vincent as their patron. I am encouraged by how many young people are coming to know and love Saint Vincent and want to share in his charism.

Vincent calls all of the members of his family to a practical, effective charity lived out in simplicity and humility. Simplicity, for him, is love of the truth. It is saying things as they are, with gentleness and charity. Humility is the capacity to see all things as grace, as a gift from God. Simplicity, humility, and practical charity are wonderfully appealing qualities. That is why so many have eagerly set off in the footsteps of Vincent de Paul.

Vincent lived much longer than did most of his contemporaries. Both literally and figuratively, he experienced the darkness of many winters and the light of many summers. He came to learn that "grace has its moments" (SV II, 453). He knew how to wait until the right moment arrived. But he also knew how to push lest a ripe moment be lost. The essays in this volume touch on many of life's varied moments and attempt to shed light on them from the perspective of the life and writings of Vincent de Paul. I hope that they will assist the reader in breathing Vincent's spirit more deeply.

Abbreviations

AAS   Acta Apostolicae Sedis

C   Constitutions of the Congregation of the Mission

CR   Common Rules of the Congregation of the Mission

S   Statutes of the Congregation of the Mission

SV   *Vincent de Paul, Correspondence, entretiens, documents*, 14 vols., edited by Pierre Coste (Paris: Gabalda, 1920-25). All references in this book are to Coste's French edition. The translations, when they are not my own, are taken from the English edition of this work, *Vincent de Paul, Correspondence, Conferences, Documents*, vols. 1-6 (Brooklyn/Hyde Park: New City Press, 1985-).

SW   *Spiritual Writings of Louise de Marillac*, edited and translated from the French by Sr. Louise Sullivan, D.C. (Brooklyn: New City Press, 1991).

Summertime

It's Summer!
An Open Letter to Young Religious[1]

My dear brothers and sisters,

It is wonderful to be young. At least, most of us who have grown older think so! Young adulthood is the summer of life; autumn and winter follow only later. In the vibrant years of youth, heart, respiration, and physical strength are at their peak efficiency. Our inner drives too are fully alive: our quest for meaning, our longing for deeper relationships, our yearning to create a better future. I am writing today to encourage you who are young to enjoy the gifts of this summertime in your life, and to use them well.

Youth has many striking advantages. As the Superior General of a community, I often see these in the lives of young religious men and women. Let me describe some of them briefly.

First, *youth has drive and enthusiasm.* It is good to rejoice in youth's vigor. I can remember a period in my life when I could interview students all day long, prepare classes until late at night, be up again at five the next morning for prayer and the eucharist, and then teach a full schedule. The day arrived when I could no longer do that. But I still look back with happy memories on the vibrant energies of youth. Young people can give with zest.

And they want to give their lives to something worthwhile. They seek a cause, and when they find one they launch into it with enthusiasm. Their dreams, their hopes, their vision of the future have not yet been dimmed by bitter experiences, or failures, or the harsh fact that much of reality changes quite slowly. Young people gaze at the world's needs and believe that they can make a contribution.

Secondly, *youth has imagination and spontaneity.* Young people bring new horizons to communities. They have the capacity to envision

1. Article originally published in *Review for Religious* 55 (#4, July-August 1996) 388-95.

new solutions. They feel free from rigid categories or structures that have become encrusted over the years. They find it easy to identify with the words of Vincent de Paul that "love is inventive even to infinity" (SV XI, 146). They are willing to "dream the impossible dream."

Spontaneity is one of the refreshing aspects of youth. Young people say unexpected things. They often question practices that some of us older people never had any doubts about. At times we may find that their questions make us uncomfortable or defensive. But we should by no means be quick to interpret youth's spontaneity as a sign of aggressiveness; rather, it often comes from a genuine desire to seek the truth.

Thirdly, *youth is able to change.* Those of us who are older have ploughed deep furrows. It becomes increasingly harder for us to climb out of the ruts that we have dug. The furrows of the young are shallower. They can be ploughed over. Their direction can be changed, so that new waters run through them and new life sprouts up.

That is why good initial formation is so important for the young. They are pliable enough to think new thoughts, learn new ways, and create new things.

Of course youth has its struggles too, its gnawing problems. Let me dwell just for a moment on a few of these.

First, *because youth is searching, it is often uncertain about its goals or even its values.* Experience tells us that young people today have difficulty making a permanent commitment. There is so much rapid change in society and so much disillusionment with those whose values the young may once have prized, that they find it hard to decide where to sink their roots. This means that young people are often confused. They are grappling with the meaning of their lives. They are hesitant about making a definitive commitment.

One of the greatest challenges in ministry today is to present attractive alternatives to young people and accompany them in the difficult task of deciding.

Several recent studies point out that young people are seeking:

- explicit religious goals
- intense community life and solidarity

- explicit and worldwide service to the most needy

Young people can certainly find these goals realized in the call to follow Christ faithfully and to give themselves to the Church's preferential option for the poor.

Secondly, *young people often struggle with their sexuality.* Of course, those of us who are older are engaged in the same struggle too!

But the young experience the awakening of a strong physical drive, sexual energy, a desire for close, intimate relationships. And unfortunately the turbulent years of adolescence often do not come to a calm, peaceful resolution, but rather to a negotiated truce, and often enough the war soon breaks out again!

It is helpful for those of us who live in community to recognize that this is a basic human story, not just ours. It is also important for the young to speak, with great simplicity, about their sexual struggles with a wise spiritual guide.

Thirdly, *youth lacks experience.* This is an inevitable fact. All of us experience life's joys and its sorrows only gradually. Growth takes time. Yet there is a deep knowledge and love that come only from experience. There is gold that can be refined only in the fire.

Of course, not everyone who experiences life's joys and sufferings grows. But on the other hand, no one grows without a healthy dose of realistic experience. Our on-going formation programs must help young people reflect on their experience and grow from it.

Having said all this, let me acknowledge that I have painted with broad strokes. Some of the gifts that I have described as characterizing young people are often found in good measure in those who are older too. Likewise, some of the problems that I have briefly touched on above plague not just the young, but also their elders.

Today let me lay before you, young religious, a series of challenges. As the Superior General of an apostolic community, I find that these are the most important things in my heart, as I think of the many young men and women who are longing to live religious lives generously today. I describe them as "challenges" (I hope that you do not perceive them as mere "pious reflections"!) because my own personal experience, with its frequent failures, tells me that they are not easy to live out in depth.

Deeply Rooted in the Person of Jesus

This seems so obvious, but there is nothing more important that, as an older brother, I could say to you. "Remember," Vincent de Paul once wrote, "that we live in Jesus Christ by the death of Jesus Christ, and that we ought to die in Jesus Christ by the life of Jesus Christ, and that our life ought to be hidden in Jesus Christ and full of Jesus Christ, and that in order to die like Jesus Christ it is necessary to live like Jesus Christ" (SV I, 295). The gospels ring with this conviction: Jesus is the absolute center. "I am the way, the truth, and the life," Jesus says. "No one comes to the Father except through me" (Jn 14:6). "I am the vine" (Jn 15:6). "I am the gate" (Jn 10:9). "I am the shepherd" (Jn 10:11). "I am the light" (Jn 8:12). "I am the true bread come down from heaven. The one who feeds on my flesh and drinks my blood will live forever" (Jn 6:51).

Let me simply recall to you today the wonderful prayer attributed to Saint Patrick:

> Christ be with me, Christ within me,
> Christ behind me, Christ before me,
> Christ beside me, Christ to win me,
> Christ to comfort and restore me.
> Christ beneath me, Christ above me,
> Christ in quiet, Christ in danger,
> Christ in hearts of all that love me,
> Christ in mouth of friend and stranger.

I recommend two principal means for focusing on the person of Jesus.

The first is daily meditative prayer. Make Christ the center of that prayer, especially the crucified Lord. Engage in a well-defined period of reflective prayer each day (e.g., a half-hour) and let the Lord capture your minds and your hearts.

The second means, and it is not completely distinct from the first, is to find, love, and serve Christ in the person of the poor. They are our lords and masters. Jesus continues to live on in them in a special way, particularly in the crucified peoples. It is so easy for the "world," and for us too, to become numb to their plight: the 5.7 million people of Haiti, who have been so poor for so long that their pain is no longer news; the 2.5 million Bosnian refugees who are victims of "ethnic cleansing"; the 1.5 million Somalians on the edge of death by starvation; the countless Rwandans who have been brutally slain. Our contemplation of the crucified Lord cannot remain merely a pious exercise; nor can it be simply meditation on a past event. The Lord lives on in his members. He is crucified in individual persons and in suffering peoples. The call is to see him and to serve him there. "When I was hungry you gave me to eat. When I was thirsty you gave me to drink. When I was naked you clothed me" (Mt 25:35-36).

Learning from the Poor, and Serving Them

I say this to you very directly: It is only the simple and humble who really grow in the Lord's life. Only they can learn the depths of God's wisdom. The saints knew this very well because they had made the gospel teachings their own. That is why the founders of communities urge all their members to grow in simplicity and humility. Learn especially from the poor. They can teach all of us about gratitude for small gifts, about patience in waiting, about hoping against hope, about loving those around us, even in the midst of suffering and oppression, about sharing the little that we have with our brothers and sisters.

It is only when we have learned from the poor that we can be inventive in serving them. It is they who will explain to us their deepest needs, so that we can bring to them gifts that will really be helpful. Your creativity and imaginativeness as young people will be nourished by what you can learn from them. They will be a life-giving source in your on-going formation.

I encourage you to drink deeply from other sources of on-going formation too. As the poor reveal to you their needs, seek to be as competent and as creative as possible in their service. Make a firm commitment to being continually formed in an integral way: spiritually, humanly, apostolically, within a community that lives and prays in the Spirit.

Freedom in the Lord

Jesus acts with wonderful freedom in the gospels. He cures on the Sabbath, much to the chagrin of the Pharisees. He moves readily from place to place in a mobile ministry. He speaks the truth without fear. He wants his followers also to enjoy this "glorious freedom of the children of God" (Rm 8:21).

A sign of freedom is your vows. They really free you to be at the service of the poor, to be mobile, flexible, available. They liberate you from a dependence on material things that binds you to one place or to one style of life. They free you to love the Lord and his people in an all-embracing way that transcends attachment to a single person, even attachment to having your own offspring, so that you might go anywhere and serve God's people with liberty. They free you even from wanting to do your own thing, so that you will be able to listen to what the Lord is asking through the calls of the poor, the calls of the Church, the calls of your community. They free you to give your whole life, even to the end, in single-minded service, especially to the poor.

Another sign of freedom, and one that I have often seen in good people, is great honesty. Jesus liberates us to speak the truth. In recent weeks I have been reading the secret diary of Cardinal Mazarin, the prime minister of France in the mid-seventeenth century, when Vincent de Paul was organizing works among the poor and was training the clergy. In his diary Mazarin counts Vincent among his enemies. And why? Because Saint Vincent spoke the truth to the queen, whom Mazarin was trying to dominate. Vincent was fearless in that regard. He was prudent. He was gentle. He was charitable. But he knew how to speak the truth clearly. In that sense, he was truly free, as were so many saints.

Real freedom involves a love that a modern writer has called "reckless but disciplined." It is "reckless" because it knows no bounds. It cannot be tied up. It breaks the chains that attempt to hold it back. But it is at the same time "disciplined," because it knows that real freedom needs to be channeled toward a single goal. I encourage you, as young religious, to dare great things and to work with discipline at achieving them.

Ministry to Other Young People

Although the elderly often have many gifts to offer to the young, it is clear that you who are young have special gifts for ministering to other young people. Today I urge you to make ministry to the young one of your principal objectives. The young are the future of the Church. They are the servants of the poor of the twenty-first century. They are searching for ways to give their lives generously. One of the great challenges that lies before the Church is to offer the young a relevant, attractive, and worthwhile way of giving their lives to God in the service of the poor.

Let me suggest three concrete means by which you who are young religious can gather other young people together:

Youth groups

Create youth groups everywhere you serve, especially in parishes. The parish is the initial and the most likely center for nourishing the faith of the young. If parishes fail in this task, the Church grows weak at its grass roots. These groups can offer a well-articulated program of formation to young people, a spirituality in the service of the poor. I know groups, sponsored by my own community, that are already very numerous and are growing rapidly. They have 46,000 members in Spain alone; 7,000 in Mexico. I encourage you to gather young people together in a similar way. There will surely be variations in the mode of formation in various countries and in the kinds of service that these groups undertake. Feel great freedom in adapting the values and structures of groups to different cultures.

Service volunteers

Many young people are eager to give a year or two of their lives in the service of the poor. Look for ways in which you can provide them with opportunities for doing so, along with good supervision and personal accompaniment. If young people are well formed to engage in such experiences, they will enjoy the opportunity of a lifetime. Their lives will never be the same afterwards. These experiences can open the hearts of the young to a deep love for the poor and a practical ongoing commitment to serve them.

Schools of ministry

Today the Church emphasizes the wide variety of ministries that are possible within the Christian community. It is important to provide good formation to young people so that they might begin to engage in these ministries early in their lives. Many young people will be eager to be acolytes, lectors, ministers of the eucharist, music ministers, catechists, liturgical artists, visitors of the sick, peer ministers.

Rooted in the Scriptures

The word of God never fails. It is effective and creative. It runs beyond mere pragmatic "calculation" and unfolds a deeper wisdom that lies hidden in the mystery of God's love. I encourage you to know the scriptures and, like Mary the mother of Jesus, to turn God's word over again and again in your hearts, treasuring it. The scriptures are water that gives us life, as Isaiah (55:10-11) puts it, when our hearts and minds are dry. They are a hammer for us, as Jeremiah (23:29) puts it, when we are complacent, too set to budge. They are food that is sweeter than honey, as the Psalmist (19:11) puts it, when we are hungering to know what God is asking for us. They are a two-edged sword, as the author of Hebrews (4:12) puts it, so that when we preach to others, it cuts into us too. In knowing the scriptures, we know Jesus himself. So, read the word of God daily. Let it be your rule of life.

My young brothers and sisters, I offer you these thoughts in this summertime of your life. I pledge you my own support as you journey through these exciting years. I write you this letter, and assure you of my prayer, as a sign of that support.

Pope Paul VI said at the end of Vatican II that the strength and charm of youth is "the ability to rejoice with what is beginning, to give oneself unreservedly, to renew oneself, and to set out again for new conquests."[2] Use these gifts well. Dream youth's dreams, but also work hard at making them come true. Pray with passion, but let the peace of the Lord penetrate you too. Reach out to the young yourselves, and help them to see and know Christ who is working in your lives. And I pray that the Lord, even later in the autumn and winter of life, will continually renew the joy of your youth (cf. Ps 42:4).

2. Closing Message of Vatican II, *Acta Apostolicae Sedis* 58 (1966) 18.

Wintertime

On Selling the Chalices[1]

Recently I received a very touching letter from a priest. He thanked me for writing frequently on the *missionary* nature of our Congregation, the Vincentians (or the Congregation of the Mission) and encouraged me to keep urging the members to renew this spirit among us. But he also told me, with great simplicity, that this creates a problem for him personally. To illustrate the problem, he cited an article that I recently wrote.[2] In describing the flexibility needed of a missionary I stated: "This means that the members of the Congregation will be agile, quick to move when needs arise." But what about the elderly? This confrere, who senses his own lessened energies and sees himself as "retiring" little by little from much of what he was formerly able to do (though, actually, he remains quite active!), encouraged me to write something on a "Vincentian spirituality for the aging." Using the database that he had at his fingertips, he reminded me that 17.1% of the bishops, priests, and brothers of the Congregation are seventy-five years of age or more; about 21% of our sister community, the Daughters of Charity, are also seventy-five years old or more.

I liked this letter very much. It moved me to examine the writings of Vincent de Paul from a very different point of view, and to reflect in prayer about those men and women who have given so much for so long and are now experiencing declining energies.

I offer the following thoughts as a response to this generous confrere. I hope that he, with others, might find them helpful.

---

1. Article originally published in *Review for Religious* 55 (#2, March-April 1996) 171-84.
2. "On Being a Missionary," *Vincentiana* XXXVIII (1994) 319.

Saint Vincent's Thoughts on Aging Members

The aging are to be loved and treasured

Vincent showed great concern that sick and aging members would be treated well. He tells the Daughters of Charity that it would be a great injustice not to do so (SV X, 375). He urges the aging not to be discouraged when they cannot do everything that the other members are capable of doing. "The Company is a mother," he tells them, "who knows well how to distinguish among those of her children who are sick and those who are well" (SV X, 375). Just as a mother treats her sick child with tenderness and compassion, so also should the Company act toward the sick and aging.

The Company should so treasure its aging members that it should be willing to make significant sacrifices in order to care for them lovingly. "I would be delighted," Saint Vincent writes to Pierre Du Chesne, "if word were sent to me from somewhere that someone in the Company had sold chalices for that purpose."[3] He writes that nothing should be spared in order to care for the sick well (SV VI, 372). The sick are, in fact, a blessing for the Company (SV VII, 179).

Witness to Fidelity and Holiness

The elderly owe the young an ongoing, deepening witness to fidelity and holiness, living out the rule of the Company and keeping alive its missionary spirit.

It is surprising how often Saint Vincent returns to this theme, particularly in his later years. He states that old age should not impede us from living out the spirit of the Congregation and from doing zealously what our limited physical energies allow us to do.

Saint Vincent felt that the elderly owe it to the Company to live out the main lines of its rule as long as they can. He was particularly insistent that they take part in the spiritual exercises of the community (SV V, 622).

---

3. SV I, 531; cf. also the conference of December 5, 1659, "We should sell the church's chalices to take care of them!" (SV XII, 410).

He speaks very forcefully to aging sisters who give bad example to the young. He tells them that, because they have been in the Company from the beginning, they are obliged to greater perfection:

> O senior sisters, o senior sisters, what do you do when your actions give the lie to your seniority? What will you say to God when he demands an account of all your thoughts, words and actions, and especially of those that have disedified newcomers? And I, wretched I, what shall I have to say for having given scandal to the younger sisters. You should know that seniority is reckoned not by the number of years but by virtue. (SV X, 90)

He repeats this theme very frequently in his conferences both to the sisters and to the members of the Congregation of the Mission.[4]

He also encouraged them to keep the fire of zeal burning within them (SV XI, 135). He wanted the elderly, including himself, to stir up the flame of apostolic missionary love within themselves, even to death.

Even in his old age Saint Vincent himself was filled with a missionary spirit. In one of his most famous discourses he tells the members of the Congregation:

> As for myself, in spite of my age, I say before God that I do not feel exempt from the obligation of laboring for the salvation of those poor people, for what could hinder me from doing so? If I cannot preach every day, all right! I will preach twice a week; if I cannot preach more important sermons, I will strive to preach less important ones; and if the people do not hear me, then what is there to prevent me from speaking in a friendly, homely way to those poor folk, as I am now speaking to you, gathering them around me as you are now? (SV XI, 136)

He hopes that the elderly will arrive at genuine freedom. He tells the members of the Congregation of the Mission, that there are old sick confreres who have asked to be sent to the foreign missions in spite of serious illness. These are people who are truly free, he comments (SV XII, 241).

Basically, he wants the members of his Company to die in battle

---

4. Cf. SV VII, 168; X 29, 46-48, 78, 90, 115, 283, 371; XI 80, 207; XIII 729.

rather than in repose. "It does not matter whether we die sooner or later, provided that we die with arms in our hands" (SV XI, 413).

I myself, old and infirm as I am, should not cease to be disposed, yes, even to set out for the Indies to win souls to God, even though I were to die on the way, or on board ship. For, what do you think God asks of us? A body? Oh, not at all. What then? Our good will, a genuinely good will to seize every opportunity to serve him, even at the risk of our lives. (SV XI, 402)

A *"theater of patience"*

The elderly have much to teach us. They invite us, as it were, to a theater of patience (SV XI, 73) where we, the spectators, can see how suffering is to be borne. In them we see the cross lived out. We see faith tried in the fire, as it struggles with the ultimate human mystery, the inevitable reality of death.

He writes to a priest of the Mission:

It is true that illness, far better than health, makes us see what we are, and it is in the midst of suffering that impatience and melancholy attack even the most resolute. But since they do damage only to the very weak, you have profited from them rather than their doing you any harm, because our Lord has strengthened you in the practice of his good pleasure, and this strength is apparent in your determination to combat them courageously. I hope also that this will be even more clearly apparent in the victories you will win by suffering henceforth for the love of God, not only with patience but also with joy and cheerfulness. (SV II, 571)

He tells the Daughters of Charity that, ultimately, patience, tried by suffering, is the virtue of the perfect.[5] In that sense, Vincent states, inevitable illness should be accepted as a "divine state" (SV I, 144).

---

5. SV X, 181; cf. also, SV XV (*Mission et Charité*) 109.

Sickness and dying reveal the true depths of the person

It is easy to witness to Christ in joyous times when spirits run high, when apostolic energies are abundant, when prayer is consoling, when the presence of one's brothers and sisters in community is strengthening. But faith, and the depths of the human person, are severely tried when, in sickness and in dying, these consolations are often lacking. Death is the ultimate human mystery. Before it we are stripped naked. It is in the dying process that we must abandon ourselves into the hands of the living God.

> No state can be found more suitable for practicing virtue. Faith is exercised marvelously in illness. Hope shines resplendently. Resignation, the love of God, and all virtues find ample matter for their exercise in illness. It is when we are ill that we know what burdens we bear and what we really are. It is the probe by which you may most assuredly test and discover the virtue of any individual, whether he has much or little or none at all. One never sees more clearly what a person really is than when he or she is in the infirmary. Illness is the surest test for unveiling the most virtuous and the least virtuous. (SV XI, 72)

Saint Vincent's Own Aging Process[6]

Saint Vincent lived thirty years beyond the median age of his contemporaries in France. Given that fact, one might presume that he had a rather robust constitution. But we know from his own statements that he suffered from a variety of illnesses.[7] Struck by an arrow at the age of twenty-five he would feel its effects for the rest of his life (SV I, 4).

He frequently suffered from fevers and a type of malaria, which he called his "little fever" (SV I, 70, 110, 196, 237, etc.), and for which

---

6. Cf. André Dodin, C.M., *Monsieur Vincent parle à ceux qui souffrent* (Desclée De Brouwer: Paris, 1981); "Vicente de Paúl y los enfermos" in *Vicente de Paúl y los Enfermos* (CEME: Salamanca, 1978) 25-52.

7. Likewise, Louise de Marillac lived well beyond the median age of the time, though Saint Vincent himself makes it clear that she looked half dead for the last twenty-three years of her life! Cf. SV III, 256.

Louise de Marillac, the co-founder of the Daughters of Charity, tenderly described many remedies (SV I, 581, 587, 597).

As early as 1615, his legs began to give him trouble.[8] By 1632, he had to buy a horse in order to travel from St. Lazare, the Motherhouse, into Paris each day.[9] In 1633, a horse fell beneath him and then on top of him (SV I, 198). However, he was tireless and, in an age when transportation was limited, was capable of covering hundreds of miles in very little time. In the first half of 1649, when he was almost seventy years of age, he traveled by horse through 375 miles of western France.

But by June of 1649 he could no longer mount the horse, so, with considerable embarrassment, he began to use the carriage that the Duchess of Aiguillon had given him.[10] He also had been kicked by a horse in 1631, thrown from one in 1633 (SV I, 110, 198-99), and fell into the Loire at Durtal in 1649.[11] That same year, he just missed being assassinated.[12] The swelling in his legs reached his knees in 1655, so that he could no longer genuflect (SV XI, 207) and had to take to using a cane.[13] He had a serious carriage accident in 1658 (SV VII, 58, 60). That same year, the ulcers in his right leg produced a gaping wound on the ankle (*ibid*). He also experienced considerable difficulty with one of his eyes (SV VIII, 23). From 1659 on, he was no longer able to leave St. Lazare and within a few months he had to remain upstairs and celebrate Mass in the infirmary (*ibid*). Soon after that, he could no longer celebrate by himself and had to use crutches to move around (*ibid.*, 247-48). Six weeks before his death, these became useless to him, and he had to accept assisting at Mass from a chair (*ibid.*, 248).

As early as 1644, serious illnesses began their offensive; these succeeded in keeping him in bed for periods of eight to ten days.[14] They repeated their assaults in 1649, 1651, 1652, and 1655.[15]

---

8. Louis Abelly, *The Life of the Venerable Servant of God Vincent de Paul*, 3 volumes (New Rochelle: New City Press, 1993), Book I, 247; Pierre Collet, *La vie de saint Vincent de Paul* (Nancy: Á. Leseure, 1748), Tome I, 46.
9. Abelly, Book I, 247.
10. Abelly, Book I, 247; cf. Collet, I, 477.
11. Abelly, Book III, 267; Collet, I, 474; SV III, 424.
12. Abelly, Book III, 21.
13. Abelly, Book I, 247.
14. Abelly, Book I, 245; SV II, 481; Collet, I, 406.
15. Collet, I, 477; SV IV, 532; V, 350.

To all these maladies were added, in 1659, further problems caused by kidney stones and retention of urine. To move he had to use a rope which had been tied to a joist in his room.

In his declining years, Saint Vincent also had the painful experience of seeing his closest friends die. He was able to be present at the deathbed of Jean-Jacques Olier, the founder of the Sulpicians, who went to the Lord on Easter Sunday in 1657. "The earth possesses his body, the heavens his soul, but his spirit remains with you," Saint Vincent told Olier's followers that day (SV XIII, 166). On December 31, 1659, Alain de Solminihac, his great friend and fellow reformer of the clergy, also died. The final year of Saint Vincent's life, 1660, was marked by the death of three of his closest companions. Monsieur Portail, friend and collaborator for almost fifty years, died on February 14. On the morning of March 15 Louise de Marillac went to the Lord. "You have in heaven a mother who has much influence," he told the Daughters of Charity (SV X, 717). On May 3 Louis de Chandenier, for whom Saint Vincent had the greatest admiration and affection, also died. Vincent burst into tears on hearing the news.

All of these deaths touched the saint deeply.[16] Even as early as January 1659 he began to say goodbye to his friends. In a letter written at that time, after begging pardon for his faults, he told another friend, the former General of the Galleys, Philippe-Emmanuel de Gondi, that he would pray for him in this world and in the next (SV VII, 435-36).

Horizon Shifts Between the Time of Saint Vincent and Ours

Higher life expectancy

The statistics vary from country to country, but at present in Saint Vincent's own country, men, on the average, live twenty-three years longer than they did in his time and women live twenty-seven years

---

16. Cf. José María Román, C.M., *San Vicente de Paúl, I* (Biblioteca de Autores Cristianos: Madrid, 1981) 659-69.

longer. The average life span of religious is, I suspect, even longer. When I receive the death notices of Daughters of Charity I am continually struck by how many die in their eighties and nineties. While most of us in the United States and Europe expect to, and actually do, live to a ripe old age, such long life-expectancy was not at all the case in Saint Vincent's time.

In some other parts of the world, however, the median age of those who die is still comparable with that of France in 1660. It is therefore clear that this horizon shift applies only in certain countries.

A tendency to flee the reality of death

Of course, in the practical order, it is impossible to ignore mortality; we all die. Contemporary health care, however, is often organized in such a way as to imply the rejection of death's inevitable reality. The symptoms are abundantly evident, particularly in the so-called "developed" countries. Because of fear of malpractice suits and other litigation, doctors often keep patients on artificial life-support systems long beyond what is reasonable. Huge resources go into sustaining life in its final moments. In the United States, for example, over the last fifteen years, thirty percent of all Medicaid money has gone to patients with less than a year to live.[17]

This phenomenon too, like increased life expectancy, is limited to certain countries, since it often flows from cultural biases, the existence of significant financial resources, and litigious tendencies within societies.

But death is not the ultimate enemy. While at times we must use abundant resources and human creativity to stave it off, there are other times when we should accept its inevitable advent. The Catholic moral tradition has consistently spoken of the need to use "ordinary means" to combat illness, but it has also, in its long history, recognized that there are times when the use of "extraordinary means" causes disproportionate burdens for patients and those who

---

17. Richard McCormick, "The Catholic Hospital Today: Mission Impossible?" *Origins* 24 (#39; March 13, 1995) 651-52.

love them. The artificial prolongation of life is often the painful prolongation of dying.

The culture of youth

Linked with the contemporary tendency to deny the reality of death is a tendency to prolong and glorify youth. There is, of course, a bright side to being and remaining young. The strength and charm of youth, Pope Paul VI said at the end of Vatican II, is "the ability to rejoice with what is beginning, to give oneself unreservedly, to renew oneself, and to set out again for new conquests."[18] But the shadow side of this tendency is a fixation on the body, an overemphasis on physical beauty, and a failure to accept the aging process, with a resultant immaturity. Newspapers, magazines, television and films fill our eyes with the beauty and vitality of youth, and then often attempt to sell us the products that will keep us perennially young!

Medical advances and easing pain

In modern times, science has produced remarkable painkillers, from aspirins to total anesthesia. Now, at the end of the twentieth century, physicians can ease pain as never before. New drugs can significantly alleviate the sufferings of the sick and the dying, even if at times they have other notable side-effects, like the dimming of consciousness. At times these side-effects are so potent, that it is hard to distinguish the boundary between easing pain and hastening death.

But it is important not to exaggerate this horizon shift. Pain still looms large in the lives of the sick. Even with all the modern medical advances, in the United States for instance, there are more than 36 million suffering from arthritic pain, 70 million from wrenching back pain, and 20 million from migraines. In other words, about one-third of the population suffers recurrent chronic pain.[19] The situation is

---

18. Closing Message of Vatican II, *Acta Apostolicae Sedis* 58 (1966) 18.
19. Richard McCormick, *The Critical Calling* (Washington, D.C.: Georgetown University Press, 1989) 363-64.

surely worse in many other countries where fewer medical resources are available.

Some Reflections on Aging Today

To grow old is to possess all life's stages.
To grow old is to see God close up.[20]

Aging, like every stage of human development, is ambiguous. It can be the occasion for growth or for retrogression. I have heard younger confreres, as spectators in what Saint Vincent called the "theater" of the elderly, comment on both phenomena: "That's the way I'd like to grow old," some have whispered with a certain awe; on the other hand, with great sadness, some have lamented: "I hope I never become a bitter old man like that."

We all hope, of course, to grow old gracefully. Once, upon hearing the news of the death of a wonderful missionary who had served in China, suffered imprisonment and exile, and then lived among us cheerfully and peacefully for twenty years, a friend of mine turned to me and said: "All I want to do is clap. It's like the end of a masterpiece." In fact, I have had the privilege of knowing a number of wonderful elderly confreres during my life in the community.

In a lovely talk to the elderly sisters of the Company of the Daughters of Charity, Mother Lucie Rogé described the characteristics that she saw in faithful elderly sisters:

- a peaceful serenity
- deep charity
- a profound confidence that expresses itself in joy
- efforts at ongoing conversion that witness to a desire to live God's life deeply
- constant prayer.[21]

---

20. Jean Guitton, in the preface to Renée de Tryon-Montalembert, *L'Autunno è la mia primavera* (Bologna: Edizioni Studio Domenicano, 1990) 7.
21. Miguel Pérez Flores, C.M., "Potencial humano de las Provincias de las Hijas de la Caridad en España a partir de los 65 años para seguir viviendo ilusionadamente el Carisma Vicenciano" in *La Respuesta Exige Un Exodo* (CEME: Salamanca, 1993) 91.

I offer the following brief reflections with the hope of encouraging those who are working through the aging process. No one is ever too old, as St. Richard of Chichester once wrote, "to know God more clearly, love him more dearly, and follow him more nearly."[22]

We all grow old

Walt Whitman once wrote:

> Youth, large, lusty, loving —Youth
> full of grace, force, fascination,
> Do you know that Old Age may come after you?[23]

Today we know that preventive health care is very important. The huge decline in deaths from coronary heart disease over the last twenty-five years has come largely from improved eating habits (like the reduction of cholesterol) and the decline in cigarette smoking. It is also evident that regular exercise, weight control, and a balanced diet contribute significantly to maintaining our youth!

Nonetheless, we all grow old. Christian realism should move us to face that fact squarely. Even as I write, for example, I should recognize that, more than likely, I will be dead twenty-five years from now, if not sooner.

In a letter written to his friends on November 29, 1366, the great Italian author, Petrarch wrote, "I have grown old. I can no longer hide the fact if I would, and I would not if I could. . . . And I say to any who may follow me with reluctant steps: 'Come with assurance; fear not. . . . Age, toward which you draw amid the storms of life, is nothing so dreadful. Those who call it so have found all stages of life unwelcome, thanks to their mishandling of life, not to a particular age. The latter years of a learned, modest man are sheltered and serene. He has appeased the storms within his breast, he has left behind the reefs of strife and labor, he is protected as by a ring of

---

22. Prayer attributed to Richard of Chichester, 1197-1253.
23. Walt Whitman, *Leaves of Grass* ("Youth, Day, Old Age and Night") in James E. Miller, ed., *Complete Poetry and Selected Prose by Walt Whitman* (Boston: Houghton Mifflin, 1959) 165.

sunny hills from the outer storms. So go securely, do not delay; a
harbor opens where you feared a shipwreck.' "[24]

The evangelical challenge to grow in love

Hardly anything could be clearer from the New Testament.
Growth in love is the perennial challenge in every age of the human
person. Graceful aging, if it is truly to be grace-filled, is growth in
the charity of Christ. In community, this means warmth and gentleness towards one's brothers and sisters, whether young or old.
"For what is charity," Saint Vincent tells us, "but love and gentleness" (SV IX, 267). In an apostolic context, this means ongoing zeal,
even as one's energies are reduced and one's ability to "contribute"
is lessened.

Unfortunately, at times our self-esteem is so tied into "works,"
that we become bitter when our capacity for working is diminished.
It is crucial, as we begin to experience this temptation, to redimen-
sion our service to the poor and to the community. The elderly have
many gifts, though they are not precisely the same gifts as those of
youth. It is vital, for those who wish to grow old gracefully, to
discover those gifts and to share them generously.[25]

Maintaining a "young heart"

Cicero once wrote:

> I like a young person in whom there is something of the old.
> So also do I like an old person in whom there is something of
> the young. Someone who follows this maxim will perhaps be old
> in body, but he will never be old in mind.[26]

We often describe the qualities of youth as enthusiasm, imagination, the ability to change. But these characteristics are by no means
exclusive to the young. One of the most enthusiastic missionaries I

---

24. Petrarch, a letter to his friends, written from Pavia, November 29, 1366 or 1367.
25. Miguel Pérez Flores, C.M., "Potencial humano . . ." in *La Respuesta Exige Un Exodo*, 81-100.
26. Cicero, *De Senectute, De Amicita, De Divinatione*. Translated by W. A. Falconer (Cambridge, Mass.: Harvard University Press, 1979) 47.

ever met was an eighty-year-old confrere with whom I spent several days in Nigeria. Two of the most creative councillors whom I ever met were wise, experienced men who were well into their seventies, who could envision solutions to problems that few others could formulate. And, in regard to the ability to change, I have seen priests and Sisters launch into new careers when they were already "retired," and I have then seen them serve even more joyfully and creatively than ever before. Such people pass on a wonderful legacy to those who follow. D. H. Lawrence once wrote:

> When the ripe fruit falls
> its sweetness distils and trickles away into the veins of the
> earth.
>
> When fulfilled people die
> the essential oil of their experience enters
> the veins of living space, and adds a glisten
> to the atom, to the body of immortal chaos.
>
> For space is alive
> and it stirs like a swan
> whose feathers glisten
> silky with oil of distilled experience.[27]

Developing our contemplative dimension

We can "do" less as our physical energies diminish, but we can surely develop other dimensions of our humanity. Of special importance among these, particularly for those who "give themselves to God in the service of the poor,"[28] is the contemplative dimension of our existence. While at earlier stages in life we might find ourselves putting the emphasis on the second part of Saint Vincent's oft-repeated phrase (to give ourselves to God *in the service of the poor*), in

27. D. H. Lawrence, "When the Ripe Fruit Falls," 1929 in Thomas R. Cole and Mary G. Winkler (eds.), *The Oxford Book of Aging* (New York: Oxford University Press, 1994) 76.
28. Cf. SV I, 185; II, 64; III, 149; IV, 15, 67, 117, 126, 138, 156, 233, 280, 361, 577, 596; V 83, 107, 233, 326, 425, 584, 634; VII 13, 38, 369; IX 13, 26, 29, 221.

our declining years, the emphasis can very profitably fall more and more on the first part of the phrase (*to give ourselves to God* in the service of the poor).

In every era of our lives, it is important to use time well. Old age is no exception. One of its temptations is to fritter time away in excessive personal concern over one's health. On the other hand, one of the graces of aging is the gift of time in which one might seek the Lord more freely and concentratedly. The challenge for the elderly is to convert heavy hours of loneliness into peaceful moments of solitude with God and contemplation of his goodness. The elderly have time to read and ponder the Scriptures and to listen to the word of God in a new way. They have the opportunity to cry out with the psalmist: "I will sing of the loving kindness of God forever!" (Ps 88:2). The American poet Archibald MacLeish once put it this way:

> Now at sixty what I see,
> Although the world is worse by far,
> Stops my heart in ecstasy.
> God, the wonders that there are![29]

Reconciliation with the past

We all bear our scars and sins into the present. We need healing. Old age is a wonderful opportunity for reconciliation. It is a time when memories can be healed, even bitter ones, of flawed relationships with our parents, of failures in the course of our lives, of rejection, of personal sin. In dying, all of these must be placed in the hands of a loving, merciful God. It is surely helpful if this process begins long before the proximate approach of death. The sacrament of reconciliation and conversation with a genuine "soul friend" can provide wonderful opportunities for healing the sins and open wounds of the past. Likewise, the sacrament of the anointing of the sick, celebrated with faith, in company with one's brothers and sisters, can lead to the integral healing and peace that is the goal of on-going conversion.

---

29. Archibald MacLeish, "With Age Wisdom," 1952 in Cole and Winkler, *Oxford Book of Aging*, 302.

Loneliness

As the existentialists remind us, loneliness is part of the ongoing challenge of human existence. From the time of our sudden separation from the warmth of the womb to the time of our final separation from the family of the living, young and old, single and married experience it. It has its special twists in adolescence, in mid-life, and in the declining years. Widows and widowers experience it painfully. Celibates too taste its bitterness in their own special way.

The aging will inevitably feel deeply, as Saint Vincent did, the death of their friends. It stings terribly and adds poignantly to feelings of loneliness.

Our own dying is the ultimate experience of loneliness. We face separation from all those whom we have known and loved and who have given us their affection and company throughout the years. We are called, in faith, to rest in the arms of the living God. Death is the ultimate act of faith. In it, Jesus calls us to say with him: "Father into your hands I commend my spirit" (Lk 23:46).

We do not die alone

From the time of baptism we profess this brief, clear article of faith: "We believe . . . in the communion of saints." Hopefully we experience in our aging and in the dying process that we are surrounded by those who love us within the Community. It helps to know also that many of those who have "gone before us with the sign of faith" await us in the heavenly banquet.

I remember, a number of years ago, walking around our major seminary property with Brother Laurence Masterson. He wanted to speak that night about what heaven was like. I recall vividly how much we talked about the "banquet" image in the New Testament. We envisioned being there rejoicing in the Lord, and laughing, eating, and drinking with many of the friends whom we had known and loved in life. Shortly after that, Brother Laurence died unexpectedly. I have always thought of him since then, smiling at the banquet table, holding a seat in waiting for us, his friends.

Responding to death from within the Paschal Mystery

Jesus' death provides the model for his followers; it is the source of strength for entering into the dying process as he did. Saint Vincent was very well aware of this. "Remember Father," he writes to Antoine Portail, "that we live in Jesus Christ by the death of Jesus Christ, and that we are to die in Jesus Christ by the life of Jesus Christ, and that our life ought to be hidden in Jesus Christ and full of Jesus Christ, and that in order to die like Jesus Christ it is necessary to live like Jesus Christ" (SV I, 295). The gospel narratives of Jesus' dying call his followers to entrust themselves to the power and providence of God, to forgive those who have injured them, to place their loved ones in the hands of others, to believe that God can raise the dead to life.

In sickness and old age, a renewed, deepened understanding of our eucharistic participation in the death and resurrection of the Lord can lead us to a deeper immersion in the Paschal Mystery, as we grow in gratitude for God's faithful love and as we enter into the dying of the Lord as the source of his risen life.

I hope that these reflections are helpful to my aging brothers and sisters, who have contributed so much to my own life and to that of the poor. In an era that at times overemphasizes the need to stay young, I am reminded of Harriet Beecher Stowe's lovely description of Rachel Halliday, written more than a century ago:

> Her face was round and rosy, with a healthful downy softness, suggestive of a ripe peach. Her hair, partially silvered by age, was parted smoothly back from a high placid forehead, on which time had written no inscription, except peace on earth, good will to men, and beneath shone a large pair of clear, honest, loving brown eyes; you only needed to look straight into them, to feel that you saw to the bottom of a heart as good and true as ever throbbed in woman's bosom. So much has been said and sung of beautiful young girls, why don't somebody wake up to the beauty of old women?[30]

---

30. Harriet Beecher Stowe, *Uncle Tom's Cabin*, 1852 (New York: E. F. Dutton & Co., 1955) 138-39.

Advent Time

Advent Letters

There is an Advent spirit in the heart of every human person. It is one of longing, of yearning for a fulfillment that somehow lies beyond ourselves. It flows from our deeply rooted human incompleteness. Augustine uttered the classic description of this spirit: "You made us for yourself, O Lord, and our hearts are restless until they rest in you." All of us long for something more, as we make our pilgrim way. Even when human sinfulness pulls people to focus on power, pleasure, fame, or financial prosperity, they often find themselves moving aimlessly, without fulfillment. "Our hearts are restless until they rest in you."

Advent celebrates human yearning. It is the season of "the poor in spirit." Mary epitomizes its meaning. She knows her incompleteness. She longs for the coming of the Lord.

The New Testament makes it clear that only the humble, like Mary, receive the Lord in his coming; the proud resist him. Saint Vincent fully absorbed this truth and asked our Company to make it its hallmark. He saw humility not just as an interior virtue that would help us toward personal perfection; he described it as a missionary virtue that is utterly necessary in the service of the poor. "Let us work hard at acquiring virtue and principally humility, yes humility. Let us ask God constantly that he be pleased to give this virtue to the little Company of the Mission. Humility, yes humility, I repeat it, humility" (SV XI, 389).

May I suggest to you two Advent reflections on humility, this virtue so important to Saint Vincent:

1. It is the ground for great confidence. The humble recognize their own gifts and their own limitations. They confess their own sinfulness, but with "exuberant confidence" (SV III, 279), as Saint Vincent put it, in the power of God. In the face of apostolic difficulties—even problems that seem insurmountable—they pro-

claim with Mary: "He casts down the mighty from their thrones and lifts up the lowly. He fills the hungry with good things; the rich he sends away empty" (Lk 1:52-53). Do we have the capacity of the humble to hope against hope as we view the oppressed in China, the war-stricken in former Yugoslavia, the starving in Somalia or in other parts of the world, the drug-users, the AIDS victims, the street people in the inner-city? Do we who have seen the Iron Curtain drawn back and the Berlin Wall crumble, believe that the power of God, working in us, can cause other walls to fall down, as did those of Jericho? Are we humble enough to believe that he who is mighty can do great things?

2. Humility is the ground for enormous freedom. The humble recognize that "all good which is done by them comes from God" (SV I, 182). Power, prestigious positions, the praise of others, wealth—all these mean little to the humble. They enjoy great liberty, great mobility. When they perceive that God calls them from one place to another, they move on with hope, neither clinging to the past nor seeing their own role there as indispensable. They put their store not in the esteem of others (though they accept this when it comes), nor in the importance of their position (though they may exercise quite important posts), but in the name of our Lord Jesus Christ. Can we, like the poor in spirit, move freely where the Lord calls us? I think of Mary and Joseph in the Infancy Narratives. "Mary set out, proceeding in haste into the hill country" (Lk 1:39). "Joseph got up and took the child and his mother and left that night for Egypt" (Mt 2:14).

May the Lord bring you all abundant peace this Christmas.

1993

A rich cast of Advent characters appears on the gospel stage: Isaiah the prophet, Elizabeth, Zechariah, John the Baptist, Joseph, and the Virgin Mary. They symbolize and speak for the poor of Israel. Last year at this time I reflected briefly with you on Mary's role in the coming of the Lord. Today let me focus on John the Baptist.

Some aspects of John's life are surely not easy to imitate; they might even repel us. He lived in the desert. He ate grasshoppers and wild honey. He wore a camel's hair garment, with a leather belt around his waist (Mk 1:4-6). He fasted habitually and drank little (Lk 7:33).

Yet there was something wonderfully attractive about him. Even Herod, who killed him, found John fascinating (Mk 6:20). He hung upon his words, though he felt their sting. But John's highest accolades come from Jesus himself, who calls him a "brightly shining light" (Jn 5:35) and declares that he was the greatest person history had ever seen (Lk 7:28).

Classical treatments of "the holy" describe it as fearsome and fascinating at the same time. That was surely the case with John the Baptist. His enemies were stunned, repelled by his words. But both friend and enemy were fascinated by him.

Let me share with you three reflections about this great man.

1. John knew the Advent secret: He focused his whole life on the coming of Jesus. "I am not the Christ. Another comes after me. He must increase. I must decrease" (cf. Jn 1:20; 3:30). He realized that his all-consuming vocation was to prepare the way of the Lord.

Our own vocation is very similar. Saint Vincent tells us that the person of Jesus must be absolutely central in our lives, as it was for John the Baptist. As Vincentians we dedicate our whole lives to following Christ. We seek to share in his love and reverence for the Father and his compassionate and effective love for the poor. With him we trust in God's providence, which rules over all. For Vincentians, as for John the Baptist, there is nothing else but Jesus.

Yet we contemplate Jesus not only in his own person, but also as he reveals himself to us in the person of the poor. Sometimes he is hard to see there. Sometimes initially, Saint Vincent tells us, we may find him repelling, "but turn the medal and you will see by the light of faith that the Son of God, whose will it was to be poor, is represented to us." (SV XI, 32). Do we meditate on the person of Jesus daily, as Saint Vincent recommended? Do we see him in the starving people of Somalia, in the street people of our large cities, in the victims of violence in the first, second and third worlds?

2. John the Baptist's life makes it very clear that the following of Christ involves a demanding asceticism. John knew how to die. He

knew how to speak the truth even when it cost dearly. He knew how to focus attention not on himself but on the Lord whom he served. He knew how to engage in an active public ministry to which crowds flocked, but also how to withdraw into the desert for prayer and penance. He was able to bear peacefully both popularity and prison.

Saint Vincent too recognized the need for a demanding asceticism in the following of Christ. He returned to this theme again and again. He writes to Jean Barreau: "There is no better way to assure our eternal happiness than to live and die in the service of the poor within the arms of providence, and to deny ourselves by following Jesus Christ" (SV III, 392). He tells Antoine Durand: "You must empty yourself in order to put on Jesus Christ" (SV XI, 343).

No one, of course, likes to die. But John the Baptist makes it very clear that we will live genuinely for Christ only if we are willing to die for him. Only the person who is practiced in the art of daily dying will be able to hand himself over to God in an act of final resignation, as John the Baptist did. Daily dying consists in pouring out one's energies in the service of the poor, in listening attentively, in praying faithfully, in living harmoniously with others, in seeking reconciliation, in doing penance, in renouncing anything that is an obstacle to the following of Christ. John the Baptist calls us to prepare the way of the Lord by eliminating from our lives whatever impedes his coming.

Let me suggest that today, for us members of the Vincentian Family, an asceticism like that of John the Baptist might take these forms especially: rising early to praise God and strengthen our brothers and sisters in daily prayer; employing moderation and a critical sense in using television and other media; withholding divisive words and negative criticism; being disciplined and balanced in what we eat and drink; working hard, as servants do, for our "lords and masters," the poor.

3. A final thought about John the Baptist. The backdrop for the infancy narratives is one of joy. Luke puts the accent on Advent joy by telling us that the infant John leaps in his mother's womb at the coming of the Lord (Lk 1:41). In another context the adult John states unequivocally: "The groom's best man waits there listening for him and is overjoyed to hear his voice. That is my joy and it is complete"

(Jn 3:29). A clear focus on Christ the evangelizer of the poor with the aid of an asceticism like that of John the Baptist will fill us with joy. That will surely be a striking sign to others that the kingdom of God is really at hand.

I wish you the blessings of Christmas and the joy of the Lord.

1994

I love Advent. I have often asked myself why. The reason, I think, is that it symbolizes our human condition. We long. We hope. We rejoice in what we have. We yearn for what we have not. In the northern hemisphere, where I have lived most of my life (I ask our southern members to forgive me this allusion), even nature conspires during Advent time to make us feel our human incompleteness. As the darkness of winter descends, we long for the light. As cold numbs us, we yearn for the warmth of God's love. As plants and leaves die, sometimes with a final flash of brilliance, we hope for resurrection and new life.

In the last two years I have written to you during this season about the central figures on the Advent stage: the Virgin Mary and John the Baptist. This year let me speak about another member of the cast. He is a background character, always standing there unobtrusively, singing out in a penetrating voice: "Prepare the way of the Lord. Make straight his paths" (Is 40:3). There is not a single day in Advent when Isaiah does not enter upon the stage. Throughout the entire season the Church proclaims his words at the eucharist and in the Liturgy of the Hours.

We now know that the book of Isaiah was hundreds of years in the writing. It represents the longings of Israel. I want to place two of its principal themes before you today, since they lie close to the heart of the Vincentian tradition.

1. The Lord is about to create something new. Isaiah cherishes this theme. He repeats it again and again. "See, I am doing a new deed, even now it comes to light: Can you not see it? Yes, I am making a road in the wilderness, paths in the wilds" (Is 43:19-20). He envisions the peaceful kingdom where the warring "shall beat

their swords into plowshares and their spears into pruning hooks" (Is 2:4) and where "the wolf shall be the guest of the lamb and the calf and the young lion will browse together" (Is 11:6). He foresees the day when "justice will bring about peace" (Is 32:15) and when "streams will burst forth in the desert" (Is 35:7). He voices God's promise: "Lo, I am about to create new heavens and a new earth; the things of the past shall not be remembered or come to mind. Instead, there shall always be rejoicing and happiness in what I create" (Is 65:17-18a).

The accent here is on God's initiative. It is he who will make all things new. The New Testament seized upon this theme. It tells the story of God's in-breaking into human history. Jesus is conceived by the power of the Holy Spirit and born of the Virgin Mary. He is Emmanuel, God with us (Mt 1:23). In his coming all things are new (2 Cor 5:17); he is, in fact, good *news* (Lk 2:10). From this Isaian perspective, God does everything. "By waiting and by calm, you shall be saved; in quiet and in trust your strength lies" (Is 30:15).

Recently, as I participated in the Synod,[1] I was struck by how frequently the bishops saw us, members of apostolic societies, as Isaian, prophetic figures. Perhaps the strongest emphasis of the Synod is that we are called to live among the poor as signs of boundless hope, with profound confidence in the Lord's presence, his love, his creative power. "Behold I make all things new" (Rv 21:5a). Our vows witness to that. Our hope is in the Lord, not in our offspring nor in our possessions nor in our self-determination. We trust that the Lord identifies himself with the poor and that in joining in that self-identification we are one with him.

2. The second Isaian theme is quite different; in fact, paradoxically it seems almost the opposite. It puts the accent on human responsibility. It recognizes that God's work on earth is our work too, that every gift from God bears with it a human responsibility. The Church has made this the classical Advent theme: "Prepare the way of the Lord." I ask myself in this Advent time: What are the steps that will best help us, as members of our Congregation, to prepare the way of the Lord? I suggest two things.

a) I encourage all the members of the Vincentian Family to give

---

1. This is a reference to the Synod of 1994 on consecrated life.

themselves wholeheartedly to the Church's preferential option for the poor. Having just spent a month in the Synod, this call seems utterly clear to me. Whatever choices in life others may make, ours is for the poor. Today, therefore, I ask each one to find the way to best touch the lives of the poor. I recognize that not everyone will do so directly (least of all myself!), but we should honestly identify the way in which our life and works will have a real effect on the poor, the most abandoned, in society.

b) When Mother Teresa spoke during the Synod, she mentioned that her Sisters pray four hours every day. She said this with great directness, without the slightest boast. Her talk was remarkably simple. She was telling us basically that her Sisters' lives are for God and for the poor. She said that we must love God with all our hearts and that we must love the poor. Surely, Saint Vincent felt the same way. So too, I am convinced, must we. One of the signs of our trust in the Lord, and of our self-gift to him, will be faithfulness to personal prayer daily, even in the midst of our multiple activities.

We have a wonderful vocation. I urge all the members of the Vincentian Family to use this Advent time to rekindle the fire that the Lord's Spirit has already ignited within us. We can be utterly confident that if the Lord is with us no one can be against us. If we work with the Lord—or perhaps better, if we do his work—he will make all things new. In the Lord, we have nothing to fear and everything to hope for.

Let me conclude with a final word from the prophet Isaiah: "I have called you by name; you are mine. When you pass through the water, I will be with you; in the rivers you shall not drown. When you walk through fire, you shall not be burned; the flames shall not consume you. For I am the Lord your God, the Holy One of Israel, your Savior" (Is 43:1-3a).

With you, in this Advent time, I pray that the Lord "when he comes may find us watching in prayer, our hearts filled with wonder and joy."[2]

---

2. Advent Preface II.

1995

Joseph receives little attention these days, even in Advent. I have surely been slow to think about him myself, having turned, when I wrote past Advent letters, first to Mary the Mother of Jesus, then to John the Baptist, and last year to Isaiah. But if we read Matthew's infancy narrative carefully, Joseph stands right beside Mary at the center of the stage. In fact, his is the major role in Matthew's story.

We know very little about the historical Joseph. His beginning and his end are shrouded in obscurity. The gospel stories about him are a theological portrait, painted with delicate shadings, so that we, the readers, might learn from Joseph how to walk with God. In the light of the New Testament, let me share with you, as an Advent reflection, some thoughts about this great man, whom Mary chose to accompany her through life.

First of all, he knew how to listen to God's word. Matthew tells us of Joseph's four dreams (I sometimes wish mine were as clear as his!). Through these dreams, God speaks to Joseph at critical moments in the history of Jesus. In each instance, Joseph responds immediately and does what God asks. When the angel tells Joseph not to be afraid to take Mary as his wife, as soon as Joseph awakes he does as the angel of the Lord has directed him and receives her into his home (Mt 1:24). When the angel warns Joseph to take the child and his mother and flee into Egypt because Herod is seeking to kill Jesus, Joseph gets up and leaves that very night (Mt 2:14). When after the death of Herod the angel directs Joseph to set out for Israel, he departs immediately (Mt 2:21). When he is warned in a dream not to go to Judea, he changes his route right away and settles in Galilee (Mt 2:22). In his faithful response to God's commands, Matthew's Joseph parallels Luke's Mary. Both know how to "listen to the word of God and act upon it" (Lk 8:21).

Secondly, it is clear in Matthew's gospel that Joseph stands, with eager expectation, at the threshold of transcendence. From the darkness of his own limited understanding, he is continually peering into the mystery of God. Surely he cannot fathom the virginal conception of Jesus that the angel announces, but as a "just man" (Mt 1:21) he tempers the strict observance of the law with loving compassion and bows in reverence to God's incomprehensible ways.

Surely he does not understand how this child, who seems like any other, could be "God with us" (Mt 1:23), but he abandons himself, in faith, to the task of loving the child and educating him. There is something very beautiful about Joseph's contact with the transcendent mystery of God. He was not a monk. He did not live a life cut off from ordinary daily contacts with the world. In fact, he was a carpenter (Mt 14:55), a neighborhood craftsman who did woodwork and made furniture, and he raised his son in the same trade (Mk 6:3). Yet in the midst of his daily manual labor and family life, Joseph was surrounded by the mystery of God and he penetrated it with faith. He trusted in God's daily providence. He believed in God's revealing word. When he read the signs of God's will, he rushed to put them into practice.

For those who live in the Vincentian tradition, Joseph has much to say during this Advent time. Let me offer two Advent suggestions that flow from the life of this deeply believing man.

1. Could not all of us try to renew our love for the word of God this Advent? For Joseph, as for Mary his wife, the word of God is paramount. This word, as Saint Vincent puts it, "never fails" (CR II, 1). The clearest thing about Joseph in the gospels is that he was always listening for what God wanted to tell him and, once he knew it, he put it into practice. Abelly says a similar thing about Saint Vincent: "He seemed to suck meaning from passages of the scriptures as a baby sucks milk from its mother. And he extracted the core and substance from the scriptures so as to be strengthened and have his soul nourished by them. . . . And he did this in such a way that in all his words and actions he appeared to be filled with Jesus Christ."[3] Is the word of God really central for us, as it was for Joseph and for Saint Vincent? Is it water that gives us life, as Isaiah puts it (Is 55:10-11), when our hearts and minds are dry? Is it a hammer for us, as Jeremiah puts it (Jer 23:29), when we are complacent, too set to budge? Is it food that is sweeter than honey, as the psalmist puts it (Ps 19:11), when we are hungering to know what God is asking for us? Is it a two-edged sword, as the author of Hebrews puts it (Heb 4:12), so that when we preach to others, it cuts into us too?

2. With Matthew's Joseph, I want to urge you this Advent to gaze

---

3. Abelly, Book III, 72-73.

into the mystery of God with courage. I say "with courage," because it is no easier for us to believe than it was for Joseph. Many of the outward signs that he saw seemed to contradict the promises that God was making to him. It is often that way for those who serve the poor. While there are many joyful moments in our ministry, there are also dark, fearful ones. The beatitudes tell us "happy are the poor," but we often see them oppressed and beaten down by injustice, as in Mozambique, Albania, and many other places. The word of God says that "the meek shall possess the land," but we often witness violent, even fanatical, strife that takes the lives of countless innocent non-combatants, as is occurring in ex-Yugoslavia and Rwanda. The gospels tell us that "those who are persecuted for justice's sake will inherit the kingdom of God," but we often observe, as in China, that persecution is long, painful, and discouraging. Joseph knew similar experiences. He knew the pain and embarrassment of poverty when there was no room in the inn and he had to place his infant child in a manger. He witnessed violence when Herod unleashed his wrath against children in Bethlehem. He felt persecution when he fled to Egypt with Mary and Jesus, and later to Nazareth. Yet he believed. He believed that God walked with him, that God is faithful to promises, that God is alive, that we can find God not only in the light but also in the darkness. He lived on the edge of mystery and was not afraid to gaze into it with courage in order to find God.

Advent is upon us. Imagine how Joseph felt as the birth of his mysterious son approached: puzzled, excited, awed. Yet, in his puzzlement, this carpenter of modest means had enormous resources. The word of God was his strength. Deep faith was his light in the darkness. It enabled him to see the presence of God even where suffering, privation, and violence appeared to reign.

If love for God's word and lively, penetrating faith were indispensable tools for Joseph the carpenter, they are likewise so for all of us missionaries.

I pray that this Christmas time will bring you abundant peace and joy in the Lord.

Lenten Time

Lenten Letters

1993

The roots of Lent are entwined with baptism. In Lent, over the centuries, countless Christians have made, or renewed, their commitment to follow Christ even to death. We often repeat during this season the words that Paul probably took from an early Christian baptismal hymn: "Your attitude must be that of Christ. Though he was in the form of God, he did not deem equality with God something to be grasped at. Rather, he emptied himself and took the form of a slave, being born in the likeness of men. He was known to be of human estate, and it was thus that he humbled himself, obediently accepting even death, death on a cross. Because of this God highly exalted him and bestowed on him the name above every other name, so that at Jesus' name every knee must bend in the heavens, on the earth and under the earth, and every tongue proclaim to the glory of God the Father: Jesus Christ is Lord!" (Phil 2:5-11).

The stark shadow of the cross falls over Lent, but its image is sharpened by the bright light of the resurrection. For the New Testament writers Jesus *must* not escape his hour. He *must* undergo the cross if he is to enter into his glory. His followers, too, *must* take up their cross daily. Paul glories in the cross, because in the New Testament the cross of Christ, as well as those of his followers, is always viewed from the perspective of resurrection faith.

May I ask of you two things during this Lenten season. Both of them, it seems to me, are close to the heart of the Vincentian tradition.

Meditation on the crucified Lord

The author of the first letter to Timothy tells us that the fullness of truth lies in "Christ Jesus, the self-giving one" (1 Tm 2:5-6). In fact, all Christian spirituality focuses on the crucified and risen Jesus. He is the way, the truth and the life. No one comes to the Father except through him. The cross is the symbol of what is at the core of Jesus' person: "The way we came to understand love was that he laid down his life for us; we, too, must lay down our lives for one another" (1 Jn 3:16). The crucified Jesus proclaims that self-giving love is at the heart of being God and at the heart of being human.

I encourage you to meditate frequently during Lent on the cross as the symbol of God's love. It is a practice that Saint Vincent recommended again and again. "Where do you think the great Bonaventure got all his wisdom?" he says. "In the sacred book of the cross!" (SV IX, 217).

It is most important that we ourselves experience the love God reveals through the cross, that we have a deep confidence in a personal loving God who works actively in our lives. This is the foundation for all our preaching and for all our pastoral ministry. Our own experience of God's love will move us to proclaim it as good news. This love is self-giving, sacrificial, forgiving, healing, unifying, loyal to one's friends, powerless in solidarity with the weak, and utterly confident in the power of God.

Meditation on the crucified Lord in the "crucified peoples"

Sin continues to work in our times, crucifying the Lord of history. Vincentians see the crucified every day in the streets of large cities and in poor country villages. But it is so easy for the "world," and for us too, to become numb to their plight: the 5.7 million people of Haiti, who have been so poor for so long that their pain is no longer news; the 2.5 million Bosnian refugees who are victims of "ethnic cleansing"; the 1.5 million Somalians on the edge of death by starvation. Our contemplation of the crucified Lord cannot remain merely a pious exercise; nor can it be simply meditation on a past event. The Lord lives on in his members. He is crucified in individual persons and in suffering peoples. The call is to see him and to serve him there.

One of the great gifts of our founder was the ability to recognize the crucified Christ in the face of the suffering and to mobilize the energies of others in their service. He was an extraordinary organizer. To aid the most abandoned of his time, he gathered together rich and poor, women and men, clergy and lay. As he contemplated suffering humanity, he knew, to use the eloquent phrase of a contemporary writer, that the "crucified peoples" bring salvation to us, as we labor to take them down from the cross.

In a Lenten framework, our meditation on the crucified Lord, who loves us even to death, and on the crucified peoples in whom the Lord continues to live, will always be brightened by resurrection faith. The gospel is always good news. It proclaims loud and clear that suffering love triumphs, that the power of God works through human weakness, that the light overcomes the darkness, that there is hope even in the face of hopelessness.

I hope that this Lenten time will be a period when all of us together can grow in faith in the person of the crucified and risen Lord who continues to live among us and whom we believe to be the Lord of history.

1994

Lent cries out for conversion. Right from the start, the Church reminds us that Jesus' preaching ministry begins with a call to change our lives (Mk 1:14-15). He, like John the Baptist (Mk 1:4) proclaims a baptism of repentance for the forgiveness of sin. But Lent addresses that call not to a far-off semitic people of another era; it directs it to us. Do we hear the call?

Lent, in its steady march toward Easter, focuses on the mystery of sin and forgiveness. In the creed that we proclaim on Easter Sunday, we profess our faith in the one "holy Catholic Church," but in Lent we acknowledge that this same Church is a sinful Church. The very existence of Lent bears witness to the truth that the communion of saints on earth is always also a communion of sinners, in need of continued conversion.

Modern popes, from Pius XII to John Paul II,[1] have stated that the contemporary era has lost the sense of sin. That is surely

---

1. Cf. *Reconciliatio et Paenitentia* 18.

disastrous, since it bears as its consequence a dulling of our felt need for conversion. But sin is very much alive today as in every age. It seeks to reign over us, as Paul reminds us (Rm 5:21). Let me suggest some of the ways in which it continues to work powerfully in the modern world, and certainly among us too.

1. A modern philosopher once stated that the great sin of the present age is *inattentiveness*. We do not hear. The gospels too identify this as one of the fundamental sins: "Seeing they do not see, hearing they do not hear, lest they should be converted and live" (Mt 13:14-15). With all its wonderful means of communication, does the world really hear the voices of the forty thousand infants who die each day of starvation? Does it hear the cries of the millions who are now dying in ex-Yugoslavia, Somalia, Burundi, Rwanda, and Cambodia? Closer to home, have we Vincentians really learned to listen to the cries of today's poor? Have we perceived the new needs of the clergy? Do we listen to one another? Are we conscious of the joys and sorrows of those living with us in our local community? Do we hear the voice of the humblest as well as of the most powerful?

2. Sin also shows itself in *lukewarmness*, lethargy, routine. I speak here not of the dramatic sins that everyone recognizes, and that are somehow easier to deal with, but of the slow, corrosive kind that dulls us to the vibrant call of the gospel. "How I wish that you were . . . hot or cold! But because you are lukewarm, neither hot nor cold, I will spew you out of my mouth!" (Rev 3:15-16). Sin makes us lukewarm in praying. It makes us selective in responding to the gospel sayings (implementing those I like, while ignoring those I do not like). Sin draws us to speak easily of the faults of others, to caricature them. It saps away the burning charity that would draw us to say "only the good things people need to hear, things that will really help them" (Eph 4:29).

3. Sin shows itself as *creeping infidelity*. In many places today one out of two marriages break up. Many vocations to the vowed life are likewise shipwrecked. Surely in some cases the marriages should never have taken place or the persons should never have entered communities. But in other cases, genuine commitments gradually disintegrate. They rarely break up all at once; their dissolution begins with small infidelities. As Jeremiah puts it, the gold of the temple is

tarnished little by little (cf. Lam 4:1). Abandonment of the Vincentian vocation, experience tells us, is usually preceded by gradual loss
of faithfulness in prayer, simplicity in speaking about oneself,
presence to one's brothers and sisters, enthusiasm in preaching the
good news to the poor, and fidelity to one's vows.

May I propose to you two very traditional Lenten means toward
conversion.

a) There is a wonderful Johannine text that merits much meditation during this season: "Everyone who practices evil hates the light;
he does not come near it, for fear that his deeds will be exposed. But
the one who acts in truth comes into the light to make clear that his
deeds are done in God" (Jn 3:20-21). I encourage you, my brothers
and sisters, to bring your own sinfulness into the light. Place it, with
simplicity, before a spiritual director and a confessor, especially
during this Lenten time. Identify, with great honesty, how sin works
most effectively within you. The promise of Lent is that the Lord
will heal you.

When we acknowledge our sinfulness, we stand in very good
company, because the church of sinners and the church of saints are
not two different churches. They are one and the same. Among the
heroes in this church are people like Peter, who denied the Lord,
like the sinful woman of Luke's gospel, like the woman at the well,
like the woman caught in adultery, like Zacchaeus, like the prodigal
son. The saints are sinners who acknowledge their failings, ask the
Lord's healing, and love heroically.

b) Besides penance and spiritual direction, may I suggest one
other Lenten means. If inattentiveness is the great sin of the modern
world, then we must take the time to listen. What is the Lord saying
in prayer? What are the deepest voices of the modern world utter-
ing? What are our brothers and sisters in community trying to tell
us? Listening demands quiet in our lives, since peaceful silence is
the precondition for hearing well. Be sure to set aside frequent times
of quiet prayer in this season, so that you might hear the voice of
the Lord and of those in need.

An ancient homily for Holy Saturday asks: "What is happening?
Today there is a great silence over the earth, a great silence and
stillness, a great silence because the king sleeps." The king sleeps

because he has been wounded fatally by the sin of the world, and ours as well. I encourage you to go down into the tomb with him in this Lenten time, as this ancient homily suggests, to enter into his dying, so that you might spring up with him, fully alive and renewed, at Easter time.

1995

There must be some daring in the following of Christ. Without risks, Christianity becomes bland. "If anyone wants to come after me," Jesus proclaims, "let him deny himself, take up his cross, and follow me" (Mk 8:34). Martyrs, celibates, monks, missionaries all remind us that love of the Lord engenders daring dreams.

Lent is a time of daring resolution. It speaks of a fundamental risk. In Lent we pledge our free, loving participation in the passion of Christ. We say yes to the journey to Jerusalem. We renew the commitment made at baptism to die with Christ in the hope of the resurrection. Historically, Lent has always been a moment of radical decisions: when catechumens stepped forward to follow Christ; when Christians chose to do penance for their sins; when penitents undertook the long fast.

May I ask you to dare this Lent? This challenge does not come merely from me; it echoes the New Testament. The letter to the Hebrews sings the praises of a long series of risk-takers. From Abel to the martyrs and other heroes in the early days of the Church "the world was not worthy of them" (Heb 11:38)—and it urges us, surrounded by this great cloud of witnesses, to fix our eyes on Jesus who risked the cross in the hope of the resurrection.

I suggest that we be daring, among other things, in regard to the traditional Lenten works. These works are intimately bound together in that they all aim to set us free. The proper practice of each demands attention to the others. By them, "we empty ourselves in order to put on Jesus Christ," as Saint Vincent loved to say to the Company (SV XI, 343; cf. Rm 13:14).

Fasting

Christian fasting evokes longing for the Lord's return. Through it we experience hunger, emptiness, yearning for the great heavenly feast. As we fast, we bow down before the Lord, recognizing that he alone is our fullness. Isaiah reminds us that true fasting also involves "setting the captive free, breaking every yoke, sharing your bread with the hungry, sheltering the oppressed and the homeless, clothing the naked when you see them, and not turning your back on your own" (Is 58:6-7). These are intrinsically linked with fasting because a longing for the Lord and his kingdom drives us to do the works of justice. Do many of us fast today? We know, of course, that cutting back on the consumption of tobacco, alcohol, and some kinds of food can have obvious health advantages. Do we dare to reach out for these benefits? Even beyond that, could we risk real fasting this Lent, being satisfied with simple fare and giving the proceeds to the poor, as Augustine and so many others since him have suggested.[2]

Almsgiving

There is a strange paradox in Christianity. We believe, with the author of Genesis, that the material things God has created are good; yet Jesus warns us not to let them weigh us down. Missionaries especially must be free, unencumbered, ready to go wherever the Lord sends them. Our goods are instruments in reaching out to others, especially the poor, rather than buffers that insulate us from them. Are there material things that hold me back? Can I use my goods more socially, as ways of embodying my love and service? The Lenten call is quite stark: "Go, sell what you have, give it to the poor, and come follow me" (Mt 19:21). May I ask that we all be daring in this regard too? Is there a generous gift I can give that will be an effective sign to the poor that the kingdom of God is at hand? Is there a special project that you as an individual, or your house, your mission team, your parish, or your province might undertake as Lenten "alms" to the oppressed?

---

2. Cf. Sermon 208.

Prayer

Both fasting and almsgiving flow from and lead to prayer. Dare to pray more intensely this Lent. You may, if your experience is anything like mine, find inner resistance to this suggestion: are there not "more important" things to do? Am I not often "wasting time" distractedly when I pray? But the initial Lenten gospel (Mt 4:1-11) tells us that before Jesus begins to preach he prays; before he mingles with the crowds he enters into solitude; before he seeks out the sick and sinful he contemplates the face of his Father. Since your schedule is probably already full, I suspect that your saying yes to more intense prayer in Lent will necessarily mean that you risk saying no to something else. What is it that I must set aside in order to pray more this Lent?

Sometimes, timidly, we merely sip of life. Lent encourages us to drink a deep draught. "Can you drink the cup that I will drink?" (Mk 10:38) Jesus asks. His cup is deep, filled with risks, but it is transforming. From it flow strange signs, like martyrdom, simplicity of life, solidarity with the poor, celibacy, community, missionary zeal. When we drink it, we begin to die, but we also begin to live a new kind of life.

With you, I ask the Lord to bless the Company, that we might all dare to live Lent fully.

1996

May I ask you to think about death? It is a delicate subject, I know, since death is the darkest, most fearful of human mysteries. Few of us are eager to peer into its depths. But we must not avoid reflecting on it in Lent, since traditionally the season begins with the stark admonition: Remember that you are dust and unto dust you shall return. Simultaneously, the Church, in a sacramental gesture so characteristic of Catholicism, signs our foreheads with the cross, using a graphic symbol of mortality, ashes.

Death is one of the principal Lenten themes. The cross of Christ casts its shadow over the entire season as we prepare to renew our baptismal commitment. Paul reminds us straightforwardly about what that involves: "Are you unaware that we who were baptized into Christ Jesus were baptized into his death? We were indeed buried with him through baptism into death, so that, just as Christ was raised from the dead by the glory of the Father, we too might live in newness of life" (Rm 6:3-4).

Modern society seeks eagerly to flee from the thought of death. Television commercials suggest miraculous salves for wiping away the latest wrinkle and rinses for darkening graying hair. Modern languages creatively invent euphemisms to circumvent the mention of death. People pass away, they leave us, they move on. Yet the fact is: they die. All of us do. No one escapes the inevitable mystery of death.

But as Christians, we view death with resurrection faith. Death cannot merely be a mystery of darkness for us. It is, rather, the dawning of light. We believe that death is the door to life, a new beginning. It is the immersion of the human person in the transcendent mystery of God.

Two events, both connected with death, occupy my mind this Lent. May I ask you to reflect on them with me, and may I offer you a practical suggestion in regard to each.

1. This year we meditate in a special way on the death of one of our brothers, John Gabriel Perboyre, whose canonization we will soon celebrate. Four years before his death, John Gabriel wrote: "We ought to be ready at any moment that our heavenly Father might want to call us. It is not wise to hope for long years, since a serious sickness or an unexpected death can always come upon us. Our whole life ought to be a continual preparation for a holy death."

John Gabriel recognized the truth that, even when we are living life to the full, we are always in the process of dying. He saw that it is crucial to confront inevitable death in a healthy way. Thus, the saints deal with death soberly. Saint Vincent tells us that for the last eighteen years of his life, he thought of, and prepared for, his death each day.[3] Teresa of Avila once stated that we will never do anything worthwhile unless we resolve, once for all, to accept the stark reality of death.

---

3. Abelly, Book I, 251.

My first suggestion this Lent is that each local community meditate and share its reflections on the death of Perboyre. He is so popular in the Vincentian Family because, it seems to me, his heroic martyrdom captured the imagination of so many of us from the time of formation. The people of China continue to share in his passion today, as do countless others in Asia, Africa, and numerous countries throughout the world. Each of us too must one day come face to face with the relentless approach of death, even if in a less dramatic form than Perboyre's (my own, if statistics hold true, will occur within the next two decades).

2. This Lent we are publishing a new *Instruction on Stability, Chastity, Poverty, and Obedience in the Congregation of the Mission*. As you read it, I ask you to focus on the vows as a deepening of your baptismal commitment to enter into the dying and rising of the Lord. Our vows have many dimensions, but among the most striking of these is that they proclaim our faith in a transcendent God who raises the dead to life. In vowing to live simply and to share our goods with the poor, we recognize that the kingdom of God offers greater riches than material prosperity (cf. Mk 10:28-30). In freely forgoing marital intimacy and children, we profess our belief that God can multiply our offspring "like the stars in the sky and the sands on the shore of the sea" (Gn 22:17). In putting aside our own "self-determination" in order to serve the needs of others, we trust in a new order, in which "the one who loses his life will find it" (Mt 10:39). In making a life-long commitment to follow Christ as the evangelizer of the poor, we express our conviction that the world is, in a sense, upside down, that the poor are the rich in the kingdom of God, that they are first, our "Lords and Masters."

The faithful living of the vows surely involves much dying. It is not easy to remain true to our promised word: to renounce marriage and family, personal wealth, a portion of our individual freedom. To be a servant of the poor to the very end costs us, even if it also has great rewards.

My second Lenten suggestion is this. Meditate on each of the four vows this Lent. Speak about them with others, especially a spiritual director. Find concrete ways to live them more fully and joyfully.

Lent is here once again, with its vivid recollection of the dying and rising of the Lord. The saints, martyrs like Perboyre, and the bearers of the cross today in so many countries surround us as a "great cloud of witnesses" (Heb 12:1) calling us to renew our baptismal commitment, our vows, our missionary fidelity.

I ask you to pray for me, as I will for you, that our Lenten journey together will bring us a fuller share in the Lord's risen life.

A Time for Exercising Authority

Some Reflections on Authority[1]

I have always loved the drama presented in Mark's ninth chapter (Mk 9:33f). They were on their way to Capernaum, with Jesus walking before them. When they arrived home, he turned to them and said: "What were you talking about on the way?" There was utter silence, because they had been talking about who would be the greatest. Jesus sits down, the gospel tells us, and with some frustration, I am sure, says, "If anyone wants to be the first, he should be the least of all and the servant of all."

Again and again the New Testament repeats this theme: "The rulers of the Gentiles lord it over them," Jesus tells the apostles (Lk 22:25), "but that is not the way it is to be among you. The greatest should become the least. The one who governs should be like a servant. . . . I am in your midst as one who serves."

In John's thirteenth chapter, Jesus dramatizes this important lesson through a parable in action: He washes their feet. When he has finished, he says to them: "Do you understand what I have done for you? You call me Lord and Master and that is right, because I am. But if I the Lord and Master have washed your feet, so also should you wash the feet of one another. I have given you an example that as I have done so also you must do" (Jn 13:12-16).

Few things are clearer in the New Testament than this: The superior is really to be as Saint Vincent and Saint Louise envisioned this role, that of a *servant*.

Some Theological Reflections on Authority

Ambivalence toward authority

There is a terrible ambivalence toward authority in the modern

---

[1]. Talk originally given to provincial leaders of the Daughters of Charity in the United States, Fall 1995.

world. This is especially so in the United States, though it is true in many other countries as well. Those of you who have read Robert Bellah's, *Habits of the Heart* and *The Good Society*,[2] have noted how deep the roots of individualism are in the American ethos. Americans seek to create conditions that will actualize the potential of the individual. Whatever threatens that, we distrust. Many images in American society reinforce individualism: the pioneer, the lonesome cowboy, the self-made man. In the nineteenth century Walt Whitman entitled a poem, "Song of Myself," whose first line is: "I celebrate myself."

Over against this individualism within American society, there are also strong biblical and republican strains. These flow from the religious roots of the early colonizing communities and from the revolutionary drive to build a nation. They emphasize commitment to one another, the creation of a society where there are mutual rights and obligations, justice for the poor and the oppressed.

As is evident, these two strains generate considerable tension within the American ethos, and American religious communities, today.

Authority in the New Testament

There is also an ambivalence toward authority in the New Testament. On the one hand, the New Testament speaks with great respect about civil authority and encourages Christians to obey it: "Give to Caesar the things that are Caesar's and to God the things that are God's" (Mk 12:17). Paul's letter to the Romans urges us to submit to duly constituted authority (Rm 13:1).

On the other hand, the Apocalypse regards Roman authority as the beast (cf. Rv 13), and the Book of the Acts says that one must obey God rather than human authorities (Acts 4:19).

Even with ecclesiastical authority, on the one hand the gospels affirm that Peter is the rock on which the Church is built (Mt 16:18), and the letter to the Hebrews encourages Christians to be very mindful of their authorities (Heb 13:7). But on the other hand, the

---

2. Robert Bellah, *Habits of the Heart* (New York: Harper & Row, 1985), and *The Good Society* (New York: Alfred Knopf, 1992).

New Testament does not fail to point out that Peter denied the Lord three times (Mt 26:69-75) and that Paul contradicted him sharply when he was caving in to the demands of the Judaizers (Gal 2:11f).

So it is good to have a realistic view of authority (and, for those of us who exercise it, a humble view). It can be used for good or for evil. It can have broad vision, possess penetrating insight, and make courageous decisions, or it can be narrow, defensive, and resistant to what God really wants.

All human authority (civil and ecclesiastical) comes from, is subordinated to, and is judged by God's authority.

Authority tries to discern and to mirror what God wants. But it always does so only more or less. We must, therefore, be very modest in our exercise of authority. Like those whom we serve, we too struggle to know what God wants. And even when we think that we have a clear idea of that, we could well be wrong. Only God is identical with the truth. The rest of us mirror his truth only more or less. Humility is, therefore, a key virtue for superiors.

Authority as service

In the Christian context, authority is always service. That is its primary dimension. It is not primarily honor, though you may feel genuinely honored that the group has put its confidence in you. Nor is it primarily power, though in fact you may have the legal, and even moral power to do exciting things, to make daring decisions, and to initiate inventive projects. Authority is primarily a service that enables the community to maximize its potential and to channel its common energies toward reaching common goals.

Authority and freedom

Authority "authors," creates. It frees up energies that are yearning to be released. But the freedom involved is the freedom of both the community and the individual. The real challenge is in harmonizing the two. With individuals, the challenge is often to help them name their own gifts and to maximize them in the service of the poor. With the group, the challenge is to know what our central values are, to concretize them in objectives, and to pursue them, in a united way, with enthusiasm. The service of authority is primarily to the community as a group, even if it must often be exercised in assisting individuals. Authority aims to liberate the group from whatever holds it back, to enable it to come in contact with its deepest underlying energies, and to facilitate its channeling those energies toward the service of God and his people. Authority must therefore help the group arrive at *common* judgments, *common* decisions, and *common* actions.

Listening and dialogue

God speaks to us through the world around us, especially through the poor. He speaks to us through the scriptures, through our Constitutions and Statutes. He speaks to us through superiors above us. He speaks to us through the Sisters in various houses. He speaks to us through prayer, through reflection, through dialogue.

Listening and discernment are therefore crucial. Difficult though this may be, we must hear many voices and engage in communal discernment, with much give and take, so that our decisions are enriched by the wisdom of others. We must seek to build a united vision, through persuasion rather than coercion, so that the group *as a whole* can move forward. But authority must not hesitate to inspire the group, to hold up the charism before it, to challenge it to reach out beyond itself.

Saints Vincent and Louise on Authority

Saints Vincent and Louise recognized, with utter clarity, the emphatic teaching of the New Testament: authority is service. Let me illustrate this by two striking images:

a) Saint Louise calls the Sister servant (local superior) the "beast of burden of the house" (the mule, the ass). She writes to a Sister servant in Angers:

> Enter upon this charge in the spirit of him who said that he had come not to be served but to serve. Listen to him willingly

when he tells us that those who humble themselves shall be exalted, and that the one who would be the greatest must begin by becoming the least so as to be great in the sight of God. Finally, my dear Sister, look upon yourself as the beast of burden of the house. (SW 118)

b) Saint Vincent too has a lovely image: Superiors are the breast that feeds the community.

> If a baby at the breast could speak it would ask to have its mother well fed so that it might receive food from her. The same should hold true of subjects, for superiors and spiritual guides are, as it were, the breasts that should nourish others. When the pipes of our house are broken, we have no water, and so we should pray to God that no obstacle may be found in the pipes, which are superiors and directors. (SV XI, 120)

Saints Vincent and Louise list a number of qualities that they hope to find in superiors:

a) The superior should be a mother. She should show great affection for others. She should treat them with gentleness and charity (SW 19). There should be no authoritarianism in the exercise of office, but rather deep charity and service (SW 30).

b) Still, superiors should be firm in regard to their goals and decisions, while gentle in regard to the means for implementing them. This is a theme Saint Vincent returns to frequently, particularly in his writings to Saint Louise (SV I, 292-94; II, 298, 583; VI, 613; VII, 226). His lovely phrase is that superiors should be *"suave et ferme"* (SV VII, 226).

c) Superiors have a special obligation to witness to the presence of Christ. In the famous advice that Saint Vincent gave to Antoine Durand, a new superior, he states:

> It is essential that Jesus Christ be intimately united with us, and we with him, that we operate in him and he in us, that we speak like him and in his spirit, as he himself was in his Father and preached the doctrine taught him by the Father. That is what holy scripture teaches us. It is therefore essential for you to empty yourself of self, in order to put on Jesus Christ. (SV XI, 343)

d) Superiors need prudence. In this regard, Saints Vincent and Louise suggest two things especially:

Seeking counsel. They insist that one must speak often with the members of one's council (SV IV, 35-36). Saint Vincent almost seemed to delight in telling the confreres that he had sought much advice of many people, including the lay brothers. He says, in fact, that the Sister servant should be "the first to obey, to seek counsel, and to submit herself" (SV IX 526).

He encourages superiors to *take their time* in making decisions well. He tells others that "God's spirit is neither violent nor hasty" (SV II, 226), "his works have their moment" (SV II, 453), they are done "almost by themselves" (SV II, 473, 466; IV, 122), they are accomplished "little by little" (SV VII, 216; II, 226). "In the name of God, Monsieur," he tells Codoing, "if necessity urges us to make haste, then let it be slowly, as the wise proverb says" (SV II, 276). At the same time, he did not want superiors to drag their feet. He tells Étienne Blatiron: "Let us wait patiently, but let us act, and, so to speak, let us make haste slowly in negotiating one of the most important affairs that the Congregation will ever have" (SV V, 396).

e) Superiors must be patient. In fact, he tells the Daughters of Charity that patience "is the virtue of the perfect" (SV 10, 181). He continually tells superiors "do not be surprised if . . . " (cf. SV III, 468; VI, 92; VII, 275, 296-97).

f) Finally, superiors should be good communicators. Saint Vincent cries out in one of the Daughters' council meetings on June 20, 1647, "O, my God, how necessary that is, great communication with one another. That sums everything up. There is nothing more necessary. That binds hearts together and God blesses the council that has it" (SV XIII, 641).

Some Practical Advice for Superiors

1. Empty yourself in order to put on Jesus Christ (SV XI, 343). Our ultimate goal is to know the Lord's ways and to serve the group. That will demand enormous self-emptying.

2. Seek much counsel, knowing that God speaks to us in human

words (SV IV, 35-36). Listen well. Few things are more important than listening, yet the temptation is to do less and less of it.

3. Foster good communication among your members, and between yourself and them. Make it clear that you love them. Do not be afraid to ask pardon if you offend them (SV V, 325; VII, 245).

4. In the exercise of authority, be gentle yet firm (SV II, 298, 583; VI, 613). "What is love," Saint Vincent says, "but gentleness and charity" (SV IX, 267). Be very warm and gentle; yet be very firm in carrying decisions through. Only in that way will the province reach its goals.

5. When you have done your best, commit everything into the hand of a loving, provident God (SV VII, 597; VIII, 375).

God is a father and a mother to us all, as Saint Vincent often said (SV V, 534; VI, 444; VIII, 55, 256). He relates to us personally with daily loving care. He has a plan hidden in Christ which is much larger than the daily human events that encourage us or disturb us. One of the principal tasks of superiors is to work at discerning that plan, always in deep union with the Lord himself. I want to encourage you in that task as provincial leaders. Be confident. If you listen well, the Lord will surely speak.

A Time for Gentleness

A Further Look at "Gentleness"

Gentleness, or *douceur*, is the third of the five characteristic virtues of the Congregation of the Mission.[1] It is also one of the virtues stressed most by Saint Vincent in his conferences to the Daughters of Charity. "For what is charity," he tells them, "but love and *douceur*" (SV IX, 267).

Saint Vincent uses the French word almost four hundred times in his letters and conferences, with various shades of meaning. In the Latin text of the Common Rules, to express the same concept, he uses the word *mansuetudo* (CR II, 14).

It is very difficult to translate *douceur* into English. The literal translation would, of course, be *sweetness*. But, in contemporary English, that rarely fits.[2] Today sweetness has cloudy connotations in English, especially in describing persons. While it can still be used appropriately in just the right circumstances, its usage becomes more and more limited. Sometimes it has overtones of effeminacy. One might not hesitate to say, in Italian, that a man's character is *dolcissimo*, but one would be slow to say, in English, that he is "very sweet."

"Meekness" too, while usually used to translate *mansuetudo*, does not sufficiently convey the rich overtones of Saint Vincent's use of *douceur*. Somehow it often carries with it the connotation of timidity or lack of strength. The latest English translations of the Rules, as well as of the letters, for the most part choose "gentleness," which, it seems to me, is considerably better, because it allows for stronger overtones.

The problem, however, lies not just with the translation of *douceur*

---

1. I call this chapter a *further* look at "gentleness," since I have already treated this subject, in an earlier essay. Cf. R. Maloney, "Five Characteristic Virtues: Yesterday and Today" in *The Way of Vincent de Paul* (New York: New City Press, 1992) 37-69.
2. Actually, however, *sweetness* has a rather noble history in the English language. Shakespeare does not hesitate to use it as a tender accolade: "Goodnight, sweet prince." (*Hamlet*, Act V, Scene 2, line 373.)

as "sweetness" or "meekness." In fact, it is the thesis of this article that *douceur*, as used in the Rules, letters, and conferences of Saint Vincent, has a wide range of meanings. As a result, the word that one uses to translate it (for the sake of consistency and readability in this article, I choose "gentleness") must be supplemented by a variety of other words and phrases. I offer the following exploration of the various meanings of *douceur* as a help to those who want to "put on" this virtue, which Saint Vincent regarded as so important.

Douceur as Understood by Saint Vincent

A missionary virtue

It is a mistake to think that, for Saint Vincent, the five characteristic virtues were merely a matter of personal Christian asceticism or of individual perfection. He chooses them as characteristic of missionaries. This is evident, in regard to *mansuetudo*, when Saint Vincent introduces it in the Common Rules. There (CR II, 6) he states that the missionary, by exercising this virtue, will reconcile the hearts of men and women, so that they are converted to the Lord. Since the reconciliation of those involved in quarrels was precisely one of the goals that Saint Vincent proposed for the mission (CR XI, 8), he wanted the reconciler to be able to remain cool when he mediated disputes that were hot! He states, moreover, that missionaries, beyond all other priests, are to be filled with gentleness, since their vocation calls them to serve the most miserable and abandoned in society.

There are many instances were Saint Vincent describes *douceur* as a missionary virtue. He tells François Du Coudray (SV I, 66) that recently he had been involved in the conversion of three people, but he avows that this was possible only through *douceur*, humility, and patience. He assures another priest of the Mission (SV IV, 52) that, while giving missions, one can win over the poor only by *douceur* and personal goodness. He states that this is, in fact, the reason why he has firmly resolved to recommend the practice of this virtue to the Company. When speaking to Philippe Le Vacher about work among the captives and slaves in Algiers (SV IV, 120), he encourages him to attract them by gentle (*douces*) means. He expresses his fear that the evil which the slaves are already suffering in their captive state, joined with the rigor that Le Vacher would like to exercise, might lead them to despair.

In 1652 Etienne Blatiron, the superior in Genoa, asked Saint Vincent several times to send Monsieur Ennery to give a mission in Corsica. Saint Vincent refused (SV IV, 449), stating that Ennery is not gentle enough for that region, "where the people are uncouth and used to being rough." He emphasizes the missionary value of gentleness: "They must be won over by *douceur* and cordiality, for evils are cured by the contrary."

Saint Vincent likewise tells the Daughters of Charity that nothing conquers the hearts of those who are angry or bitter more than *douceur* (SV IX, 261).

Finally, in the principal conference that he gave on gentleness, on March 28, 1659, Saint Vincent states emphatically that it is the virtue of "a true missionary" (SV XII, 189). In another conference given five months later on the five characteristic virtues, he underlines how essential gentleness is in dealing with poor, often ignorant, country people (SV XII, 305).

Controling anger and channeling it properly

This is the principal theme of the conference that Saint Vincent gave on March 28, 1659 (SV XII, 182ff). Here he states that gentleness involves various steps. The first step has two stages. In the first stage a person represses the spontaneous movement that he feels toward anger, trying to remain calm and reasonable. This is difficult, Saint Vincent tells his listeners, but it is possible, since, while the movements of nature precede those of grace, grace can conquer them. The second stage consists in directing one's anger appropriately. It may at times be important to correct, to chastise, to reprove, just as Jesus did with his disciples. In such instances the missionary should act not because he has been overcome by anger, but because he has become its master.

Saint Vincent states that the gentle are constant and firm. They are able to think straight. On the contrary those who allow themselves to be carried away by anger and passion are ordinarily inconstant (SV XI, 65). In addition he states: "I think that the ability to discern things is granted only to those who have *douceur*" (SV XII, 190).

Respect for the human person

Saint Vincent often links gentleness and respect.[3] He tells the Daughters of Charity that there is no such thing as charity without gentleness and respect for the other (SV IX, 260). He urges Robert de Sergis to treat the domestic help gently, cordially, and with profound respect (SV I, 354).

In a conference to the Daughters of Charity, given on August 19, 1646, on "The Practice of Mutual Respect and of *Douceur*," Saint Vincent encourages them to give themselves to God by respecting one another. He notes that this will not be easy, and for that reason asks them to join with him in a prayer:

> O my God, I desire from the bottom of my heart to be gentle and respectful toward my sisters in order to please you, and once more I give myself entirely to you to strive to acquire these virtues in a manner quite different from the way I have acted up until now. But, as I am weak and can do nothing that I have resolved to do without your special assistance, I beseech you, O God, by your beloved Son Jesus, who is love and gentleness itself, to grant me those virtues, together with the grace of never doing anything contrary to them. (SV IX, 269)

Gentleness accompanied by firmness

Saint Vincent touches on this theme frequently in his letters to Louise de Marillac and to various superiors. He often tells Louise to honor our Lord in his gentleness and firmness. In a letter written to her on November 1, 1637, he says: "If the gentleness of your spirit needs a dash of vinegar, borrow a little from our Lord's spirit. O Mademoiselle, how well he knew how to find a bittersweet remark

---

3. Cf. SV I, 88; VII, 590-91; VIII, 227; IX, 260ff.

when it was needed!" (SV I, 393). In putting Monsieur Portail in charge of a mission team, in 1632, he encouraged him to honor *la douceur et l'exactitude* of our Lord (SV I, 176). In writing to the superior at Nancy, François Dufestel, Vincent tells him to be firm and uncompromising in regard to the end, but gentle and humble in regard to the means (SV II, 298). He gives the same advice almost verbatim in a letter written four days later to Jean Guérin (SV II, 300) and repeats it in another letter to Guérin four months later (SV II, 355). He returns to the same theme in writing to Etienne Blatiron, the superior at Genoa, on September 9, 1650 (SV IV, 75), as well as to Louis Dupont, superior at Tréguier, on February 16, 1656 (SV V, 552).

Using a classical axiom in a letter to Denis Laudin, on August 7, 1658, he encourages him to imitate the spirit of our Lord who is equally *suave et ferme* (SV VII, 226).

Saint Vincent summed all of this up quite carefully in his advice to a seminary director:

> We must be firm but not rough in our guidance and avoid an insipid kind of gentleness (*une douceur fade*), which is ineffective. We will learn from our Lord how our gentleness should always be accompanied by humility and grace so as to attract hearts to him and not cause anyone to turn away from him. (SV IV, 597)

Joseph Leonard, in a translation made a number of years ago, rendered this text as follows: "Namby-pamby mildness, that is useless, should be avoided!"[4]

Affability, cordiality, warmth, approachability

This is the way Saint Vincent often describes *douceur* in speaking about relationships with the poor and relationships within the Community.

Cordiality is one of the key words that he uses to describe good relationships.[5] He places it among the means for persevering in one's

---

4. Joseph Leonard, *Saint Vincent and Mental Prayer* (New York: Benziger Brothers, 1925) 177.
5. SV I, 112; IV, 51, 113, 341, 449; VI, 29; IX, 261.

vocation (SV XI, 109), stating that a missionary will persevere if he lives in deep charity and cordiality with his brothers.

He links cordiality with affability, saying that it is particularly necessary in working with poor country people (SV XI, 68). He states that affability is the soul of good conversation and renders it not only useful but also agreeable. In his principal conference on gentleness, he says that the second step in being *douce* (after controlling one's anger and channeling it properly) is affability and cordiality.

Saint Vincent is convinced that warmth and approachability are especially necessary in those who hold important positions in the Church:

> You can see by experience that an amiable way wins hearts and attracts them; on the other hand, it has been noted in regard to persons of rank who hold office that, when they are too serious and cold, everyone fears and shuns them. Since we must work with poor country people, candidates for orders, people on retreat, and all sorts of others, it will not be possible for us to produce fruit, if we are like parched land that bears only thistles. (SV XII, 189)

Joyfulness and peacefulness

Saint Vincent tells the Daughters of Charity that when someone has joy in her heart she cannot hide it. People will see it on her face. They will be grateful to God for having met her (SV X, 487).

Here, the key French word in Saint Vincent's writings is *gai*.[6] Since Saint Louise was a rather serious type, Saint Vincent often urged her to be *gaie*. As she sets out on a journey in 1631, he encourages her: "Honor the tranquility of his soul and that of his holy mother and be very *gaie* on your trip, since you have good reason to be so in the work in which our Lord is employing you" (SV I, 102). On another occasion, as she was about to travel with the more ebullient Madame Goussault, he writes: "Please be very cheerful with her, even though you should have to lessen a bit that somewhat

---

6. As all English-speaking readers recognize, *gay*, in their own language, has undergone a remarkable transformation in recent decades, so that today it very often means *homosexual*.

serious disposition which nature has bestowed on you and which grace is tempering by the mercy of God" (SV I, 502). He often recommends that she seek the peace of mind and heart that characterized the Blessed Mother and our Lord (SV I, 111, 114, 571).

During the annual retreat of 1632 he exhorted the missionaries to have great respect for one another during the time of recreation and also to be *gai*. He advises a superior to conform his conduct to that of our Lord, who was always completely humble, completely gentle, completely attentive, and accommodating, with humor, of the infirmities of others (SV IV, 581).

He constantly counsels the Daughters of Charity to be joyous, smiling in their service of the poor. He once told Saint Louise: "The kingdom of God is peace in the Holy Spirit. He will reign in you, if your heart is at peace. So, be at peace, Mademoiselle, and you will honor in a sovereign way the God of peace and love" (SV I, 114).

Forbearance and forgiveness

Support (forbearance) is the key French word here.

Vincent encourages Etienne Blatiron to treat a troublesome confrere with gentleness and forbearance (*support*), since this is in conformity with the spirit of our Lord (SV III, 383). He tells Bernard Codoing to show two confreres, with whom he was having difficulty, the gentleness and forbearance recommended by our Lord (SV III, 469). He repeats the same advice to Marc Coglée, superior in Sedan (SV IV, 51), to Louis Dupont, superior at Tréguier (SV V, 605), as well as to Pierre Cabel (SV VII, 201) and Firmin Get (SV VII, 594).

In the conference on "The Five Characteristic Virtues of the Company," given on August 22, 1659, he states that gentleness and forbearance are necessary both in community life and in the service of the neighbor (SV XII, 306). It entails enduring offenses with forgiveness and courage. In fact, we should treat gently even those who do injury to us. He encourages the missionaries:

> Gentleness not only makes us excuse the affronts and injustices we receive, but even inclines us to treat with gentleness those from whom we receive them, by means of kind words, and should they go so far as to abuse us and even strike us in the

face, it makes us endure all for God. Such are the effects produced by this virtue. Yes, a servant of God who truly possesses it, when violent hands are laid upon him, offers to the divine goodness this rough treatment and remains in peace. (SV XII, 192)

Gentleness and humility

Saint Vincent returns to this theme again and again. The Spirit of our Lord, he tells Robert de Sergis (SV I, 536; cf. I, 528), is one of gentleness and humility. In the Common Rules he cites the text from Matthew's gospel, "Learn from me that I am gentle and humble of heart" (11:29b) (CR II, 6).

In writing to Monsieur Portail about how to respond to one of the other original members of the Company, François Du Coudray, he encourages him to treat him always with gentleness and humility (SV III, 7). He assures Sr. Françoise Ménage, in a letter written on February 12, 1659, that she will become truly happy if she practices humility, gentleness, and charity toward the poor and toward her Sisters (SV VII, 455).

The Rule of the Daughters of Charity also links the two virtues, calling the members of the Company to honor our Lord particularly in his poverty, his humility, his gentleness, his simplicity, and his sobriety (SV XIII, 555). In fact, for Saint Vincent gentleness and humility are so intertwined that, like prudence and simplicity, they are "twin sisters" (SV XII, 184).

Compassion for others

Saint Vincent states that the missionary must be filled with compassion (SV XI, 77), particularly since he is called to serve the most miserable, the most abandoned, and those overwhelmed by spiritual and physical ills. He consistently links compassion with *douceur*.

In the twelfth rule for the Daughters of Charity he states: "Their principal concern shall be to serve the sick poor, treating them with compassion, gentleness, cordiality, respect, and devotion" (SV X,

331). He tells the Daughters that their holiness consists in observing their rules well and in the right spirit by serving the poor with love, gentleness, and compassion (SV X, 353).

During the conference given on July 24, 1660, "On the Virtues of Louise de Marillac," it was precisely this mixture of *douceur* and compassion that one of the Sisters noted in Louise (SV X, 727).

Saint Vincent's Practice of Douceur

In addition to looking at theory, it is always helpful to examine *praxis*. This is especially important in regard to Saint Vincent since, as I pointed out in an earlier article on the vows,[7] he shows a remarkable flexibility in applying principles to concrete situations. Moreover, Saint Vincent's *praxis* provided a context within which the members of the Congregation of the Mission and the Daughters of Charity interpreted what he said. When he spoke or wrote about *douceur*, his audience depended not only on his words as an instrument of interpretation, but also on his life.

His own self-understanding

Saint Vincent himself witnesses that when he was young he was strong-willed and easily moved to anger. He also had a tendency to be moody for long, dark periods which, he attests, caused Madame de Gondi some pain at times. But, recognizing these traits within himself, "I turned to God and begged him incessantly to change my dry, contentious manner and to give me a warm, *doux* spirit, and by the grace of our Lord, and with the little bit of attention that I gave to holding back the movements of nature, I have somewhat changed my dark moods."[8]

Saint Vincent speaks with considerable modesty here. Abelly, his first biographer, attests that Vincent had an enormous admiration for Francis de Sales, whom he considered the gentlest person he had ever known. He adds that Saint Vincent profited so well from the

---

7. R. Maloney, "The Four Vincentian Vows: Yesterday and Today," *Vincentiana 34* (Rome: Curia Generalitia, 1990) 230-307.

8. Abelly, Book III, 177-78.

example of the Bishop of Geneva that he acquired a remarkable *douceur* and affability and had a wonderful way of speaking and relating with all different kinds of persons.[9]

In fact, he learned the lesson of *douceur* so well that he was often compared with Francis de Sales in that regard. Collet observes that his gentleness and affability became proverbial and that people said the same things about him that he himself said about Francis.[10]

His respect for persons and his support of those who were difficult

The recently published notes of Br. Louis Robineau, which Abelly used in preparing his biography of Saint Vincent, give many examples of the enormous respect that Saint Vincent showed toward persons of various conditions in life, from the most powerful to the weakest in society.[11] Robineau notes especially the gentleness with which he admonished others and the profound respect with which he treated the poor. He recounts many stories too about Saint Vincent's *support*.[12] He comments that Vincent had a remarkable ability to endure difficult situations: the calumnies of others, the trials that he endured as a member of the Council of Conscience, the gossip suggesting that he had witnessed a secret marriage between Anne of Austria and Mazarin,[13] the troubles that several confreres created for him, and his own infirmities.

His warmth and compassion

His own letters give vivid witness to his warmth and compassion. He writes to Saint Louise de Marillac "how deeply I feel your pain!" (SV I, 142). He often writes with great compassion to confreres and Daughters on the occasion of the deaths of family members or members of the community (SV VI, 444; VIII, 55, 256). Just after the

---

9. Abelly, Book III, 180.
10. Collet I, 99.
11. André Dodin, *Monsieur Vincent, raconté par son secrétaire* (Paris: O.E.I.L., 1991) 53-56.
12. *Ibid.*, 143-45.
13. For a discussion of this question cf. Dodin, *Monsieur Vincent*, 173.

death of Monsieur Portail and immediately before that of Louise de Marillac, he writes to Mathurine Guérin:

> Certainly it is the great secret of the spiritual life to abandon to him all whom we love, while abandoning ourselves to whatever he wishes, with perfect confidence that everything will go better in that way. It is for that reason that it is said that everything works for the good of those who serve God. Let us serve him, therefore, my Sister, but let us serve him according to his pleasure, allowing him to do as he wishes. He will take the role of father and mother for us. He will be your consolation and your strength and finally the reward of your love. (SV VIII, 256)

In a moment of tension between himself and François Du Coudray, he writes to the latter: "I cannot, no, I cannot express to you, my dear little Father, my sorrow at grieving you. I implore you to believe that, were it not for the importance of the matter, I would prefer a thousand times to bear the pain of this myself rather than upset you by it" (SV III, 74). When Guillaume Delville and his family found themselves in difficulty in 1646, Saint Vincent wrote: "I cannot express to you the sorrow my heart felt at this and how I would like to have suffered in your place, myself alone, what you and your family have endured. Monsieur Codoing, the bearer of this letter, will be able to testify to you how deeply this has touched me. I am sending him mainly to assure you that your troubles are my troubles" (SV II, 619).

His labors for peace

To all this must be added something that is quite striking in Saint Vincent's practice: peace-making. It appears on two levels particularly.

1) He encouraged the members of the Congregation of the Mission to work at healing broken relationships. One of the goals of "the mission" was reconciliation (CR XI, 8). Missionaries were to attempt to settle quarrels and disputes during missions. In fact, they frequently reported to Saint Vincent about their success in doing so.

2) He himself worked actively to bring an end to war. He was

deeply concerned over the ravages of war and the grief that it brought to his countrymen, particularly the poor. On two occasions he intervened personally in an attempt to bring peace to his land.

At some time between 1639 and 1642, during the wars in Lorraine, he went to Cardinal Richelieu, knelt before him, described the horrors of war, and pleaded for peace: "Let us have peace. Have pity on us. Give France peace." Richelieu refused, responding that peace did not depend on him alone.[14]

Collet relates an even more striking episode, which he takes from an account written by Brother Ducournau.[15] In 1649, during the civil war, Saint Vincent left Paris quietly, crossed battle lines and forded a flooded river (at almost seventy years of age) to see the queen and to beg her to dismiss Mazarin, whom he regarded as responsible for the war. He also spoke directly to Mazarin himself. But again his pleas went unheeded.

Some Horizon Shifts Between the Seventeenth and the Twentieth Centuries

Horizon shifts significantly influence our outlook on things. The view of Rome from the pinnacle of St. Peter's Dome is quite different from the view from the surrounding Alban hills. From both places one can pick out the Tiber, many of the same buildings, the parks, and various other sites, but from each perspective they appear quite different. They may seem smaller or larger, depending on the distance. They may seem darker or lighter, depending on the time of day or the season. From St. Peter's, parts of some buildings may be seen that are not visible from the Alban hills, since one is looking at them from different directions.

All of this is evident from a "physical" perspective. One might also say, from a "theological" perspective, that the Church surely appears quite different when perceived from my office in Rome than when seen from a *comunidad de base* in Latin America! One's horizon,

---

14. Cf. P. Coste, *The Life and Labours of Saint Vincent de Paul*, translated by Joseph Leonard (London, 1935) II, 369-70. Cf. also, Abelly, Book I, 169.
15. Collet, I, 468. Cf. SV III, 402. Cf. also, Coste, II, 447.

whatever it is, always influences one's view, bringing varied insights and different nuances.

A number of horizon shifts have taken place since the seventeenth century that affect the way one might view *douceur*. Let me try to describe several of these briefly.

1. Contemporary psychology has examined anger very carefully, pointing out the dangers of repressing it.

More than a century ago Charles Darwin in his classic study, *The Expression of the Emotions in Man and Animals*, systematically examined anger responses in the human person as compared with those in animals; he saw anger within the context of the approach-avoidance pattern that characterizes all human affectivity. In 1890 William James noted that all emotional responses have physiological aspects, heightening the person's energy in view of a further response. Since that time research into the emotions has developed considerably.[16]

Today we recognize that stored-up anger often results in considerable psychosomatic damage and frequently shows itself in unexpected explosions that hurt others. Contemporary literature examines and suggests healthy ways of dealing with anger and directing it creatively.

In recent years, scientific studies have found popular expression in numerous spiritual reading books dealing with the healthy expression of the emotions as part of human growth.[17] Superiors, and those responsible for formation programs, have become quite aware that there are many "angry people" in communities (as in other callings), with potentially explosive results. Through the discussion of the emotions, and particularly anger, during the time of formation, many communities try to deal with these problems ahead of time, in order to avoid catastrophic events later.

Studies also show that emotions, and even basic facial expressions, elicit similar affective responses from others. Happy expressions elicit happy responses; sad expressions, sad responses.[18]

---

16. Robert Plutchik, *Emotion: A Psychoevolutionary Synthesis* (New York: Harper & Row, 1980) 128-51.
17. Fran Ferder, "Never Let the Sun Set on Your Anger: Anger and Its Expressions" in *Words Made Flesh: Scripture, Psychology, and Human Communication* (Notre Dame, Indiana: Ave Maria Press, 1986) 67-84.
18. G. Simon Harak, *Virtuous Passions* (New York: Paulist, 1993) 18. This author notes (p. 25) that we begin to "pick up" emotions from people about a tenth of a second after coming into contact with them.

Reading these studies, one spontaneously recalls Saint Vincent's exhortations to the Daughters of Charity to be joyful and smiling in their service.

2. In modern times there has been a very significant revival of pacifism.

In this regard, Gandhi has had an enormous influence, with his peaceful revolution in India. Likewise, Martin Luther King, in the United States, obtained very significant advances in civil rights by non-violent resistance. James Douglass' book, *The Non-Violent Cross*,[19] which gained immense popularity, capsulized the biblical and philosophical roots of pacifist movements.

In the Catholic tradition, *Gaudium et Spes* took a carefully nuanced, yet positive position in regard to pacifism: "In the same spirit we cannot but express our admiration for all who forgo the use of violence to vindicate their rights and resort to those other means of defense which are available to weaker parties, provided it can be done without harm to the rights and duties of others and of the community" (#78). At the same time Paul VI made stirring appeals for world peace, crying out on October 4, 1965, at the United Nations headquarters in New York: "No more war, war never again!"[20] In his book, *Faith and Violence*, Thomas Merton offered a clear presentation of the theory and practice of Christian peace-making.[21] In 1983 the bishops of the United States, in a carefully prepared document, made a very significant contribution to the theory and the practice of working toward the creation of peace.[22]

3. In recent times there has been increased consciousness of the need for peace-making not only on an individual level, but also on a structural level. Here too, Paul VI made an eloquent appeal: "If you want peace, work for justice."[23] John Paul II adds: "Development is the new name for peace."[24]

---

19. James W. Douglass, *The Non-Violent Cross* (New York: Macmillan, 1968).
20. *Acta Apostolicae Sedis* 57 (1965) 881.
21. Thomas Merton, *Faith and Violence* (Notre Dame, Indiana: University of Notre Dame Press, 1968).
22. The Challenge of Peace," *Origins* 13 (#1; May 19, 1983) 1-32.
23. *Acta Apostolicae Sedis* 57 (1965) 896.
24. *Sollicitudo Rei Socialis* 10; cf. *Populorum Progressio* 77.

The groundwork for this emphasis on the need for structural change is already evident in *Pacem in Terris* (#s 89 and 91) and in *Gaudium et Spes* (#85). Paul VI takes the theme up eloquently in *Populorum Progressio* (#78) and in an address to the members of Cor Unum, given on January 13, 1972, calls Christians to commit themselves to enter into "the very heart of social and political action and thus get at the roots of evil and change hearts, as well as the structures of modern society."[25]

Today we are conscious that sin deeply affects social structures. It becomes embodied in unjust laws, power-based economic relationships, inequitable treaties, artificial boundaries, oppressive governments, and numerous other subtle structural obstacles to harmonious societal relationships. It is only when such structural obstacles are analyzed, understood, and removed that society can establish abiding, peaceful relationships.

Today there is also a heightened sense of the global community and the calamitous implications of the arms build-up. The sale of arms remains one of the major factors in the world economy. Local conflicts (in Algeria, Chechnya, ex-Yugoslavia, and in numerous other places) make the international scene at times quite volatile, with the ever-present danger that these conflicts will escalate into an "all-out war." With the widespread diffusion of arms and the frequency of their use, young people often attest to uncertainty about their future because of the possibility of nuclear annihilation.

Meanwhile, papal documents have consistently condemned the arms race.[26] At the same time, the United States Bishops' Peace Pastoral set off a broad series of discussions on the question of war, peace, and arms among episcopal conferences throughout the world.

Douceur Today

Saint Vincent's teaching about this third "smooth stone" (CR II, 6), as he liked to put it, is quite translatable into modern usage. His conference of March 28, 1659, as well as several of his letters to Louise de Marillac, contain a practical wisdom that is very relevant

---

25. *Acta Apostolicae Sedis* 64 (1972) 189.
26. Cf. *Gaudium et Spes* 81.

today. While one could say much about this virtue, I will focus here
only on four points.

Handling anger positively

Anger is natural. It is energy that spontaneously arises within us
when we perceive something as evil. It helps us to deal with evil. It
prepares us to "fight," as Darwin might put it. But, like all spontaneous emotions, it can be used well or badly. Concretely, all sorts
of people have trouble handling it well. As mentioned above, there
are many "angry people" in the world.

Uncontrolled anger, in its most violent forms, erupts into war,
assault, rape, murder, and the many crimes that make headlines in
daily newspapers. In its less violent forms, unregulated rage shows
itself in outbursts of temper, angry diatribes, refusal to talk to others,
throwing things, slamming doors, pouting, holding grudges, at-
tempts at "getting even."

As Saint Vincent pointed out, handling anger well often involves
expressing it appropriately. He himself was outraged at the plight of
the sick and the hungry, so he established the Confraternities of
Charity, the Congregation of the Mission, and the Daughters of
Charity. Anger enabled him to react with vigor and creativity when
confronted with the needs of the poor in his day. He also expressed
anger directly when he perceived evil within his communities, but
he learned to combine his anger with gentleness. He knew how to
mix the bitter and the sweet, as he told Louise de Marillac (SV I,
292-94). He sought to imitate Jesus who was equally "gentle and
firm" (SV VII, 226).

Venting a roused spirit appropriately can be very healthy. It can
ease hidden tensions and work toward the resolution of conflict. It
can be an appropriate instrument in correction. But if anger is
handled badly, it can be terribly destructive. Unleashed, it can result
in violence and injustice. Repressed, it can fester into resentment,
sarcasm, cynicism, bitterness, depression.

The challenge is to learn the ways of appropriately controlling,
moderating (even suppressing anger for a period of time), sublimat-
ing, and expressing anger. Saint Vincent often appeals to the

example of Jesus who knew how to moderate, and yet express, his frustration in regard to the apostles, and who could be very direct in expressing his anger in regard to the Pharisees, who were laying unjust burdens upon others.

Approachability, affability, warmth

These are especially important qualities in ministers. In this regard, Saint Vincent encourages us to be confident that we can really change, citing his own personal experience. While he was of choleric temperament and, in his younger days, rather moody for long dark periods, he changed so much in the course of his life that all those who knew him later said that he was one of the most approachable men they had ever met.[27]

He told the community that people are won over much more by gentleness than by argument. This advice is especially relevant when we offer the gift of correction (cf. Mt 18:15-18), whether the correction is done by peers or by superiors. Those corrected are much more able to hear words spoken gently than words of stinging accusation.

Moreover, gentleness and warmth in the giver draw out the same gifts in the receiver. Those who find the minister warm and loving will begin to respond in the same way. This is surely why Saint Vincent so emphasized *douceur* as a "missionary" virtue.

Enduring offenses with forgiveness and courage

Saint Vincent based his teaching in this regard on respect for the human person. Even those who commit injustice, he told the double Vincentian Family, deserve respect as persons. The writings of John Paul II reiterate this theme in our day — the call to have profound reverence for each individual.

Naturally, having respect for the person of the offenders does not prohibit us from channeling our anger with courage against the evils they are committing. But it does prohibit us from practicing injustice in the name of justice. Saint Vincent recognized clearly (and he reminded Philip LeVacher about Augustine's teaching in this regard

---

27. Cf. Abelly, Book III, 177-78.

[SV IV, 121]) that there are some evils that must be tolerated, since there is no practical possibility of correcting them. The wise person learns to live with them, and the gentle person treats with respect those whose lives are so entwined with evil that it cannot be rooted out.

There is a delicate balance in this regard. At times one must suffer with courage. There are evils that cannot be avoided and that must be endured. But on the other hand, one must avoid a false gentility, as Adrian Van Kaam once put it[28] (or, to use Joseph Leonard's translation of Saint Vincent's phrase, "namby-pamby mildness"!). At times one must cry out against injustice and channel all one's energies into overcoming it. It takes great prudence to know the difference between these cases.

At this time of rapid change in the history of the Church, the combination of gentleness and firmness is especially necessary. This is particularly so in making decisions. As communities assess their apostolates with a view toward the future, they must have the courage to choose and act. At the same time, they must show gentleness toward those who have great difficulty adapting. Likewise, individuals must have courage in setting growth-goals, but they must be gentle with themselves by recognizing that personal change does not occur overnight, but only gradually.

Ministers too must know that no matter how well they do their jobs, they will have to endure, with both courage and gentleness, their own limitations and the conflicting expectations of others. Religious superiors will experience that some in their communities see all things in black and white, while others love only what is grey. Some will use the past as their dominant norm for decision-making, while others will look only to an uncharted future. Superiors will never fully satisfy all these different personalities. They must make decisions with courage and treat with gentleness those who disagree. They must combine in their lives two New Testament sayings: "With the strength that comes from God, bear your share of the hardships the gospel entails" (2 Tim 1:8), and "Learn of me that I am gentle and humble of heart, and you will find rest for your souls" (Mt 11:29).

---

28. Adrian L. Van Kaam, *Spirituality and the Gentle Life* (Denville, New Jersey: Dimension Books, 1974).

Action on behalf of justice and peace-making

Today especially, witness to Jesus' gentleness and his proclamation of a kingdom of peace play a very prominent part in the
Church's preaching of the good news. This is intimately linked with
the promotion of justice and peace and education toward both.
Centesimus Annus speaks eloquently on the theme: "I myself, on the
occasion of the recent tragic war in the Persian Gulf, repeated the
cry: 'Never again war!' No, never again war, which destroys the lives
of innocent people, teaches how to kill, throws into upheaval even
the lives of those who do the killing and leaves behind a trail of
resentment and hatred, thus making it all the more difficult to find
a just solution of the very problems which provoked the war. . . . For
this reason, another name for peace is *development*. Just as there is a
collective responsibility for avoiding war, so too there is a collective
responsibility for promoting development" (#52; cf. 14, 54).

Aquinas reminds us that the passion most immediately associated
with justice is anger.[29] Anger recoils in the face of injustice in order
to spring back and wipe it out. It moves us to lunge toward justice,
to hunger and thirst for it. Anger springs from love and respect for
the human person, whose rights we perceive as being violated. It
strains to right wrong, to reestablish an order in which persons can
grow and flourish. It will always be aroused, therefore, when we
perceive that unjust structures are depriving the poor of the political,
social, economic, or personal freedom that their human dignity
demands.

Gentleness finds the ways of expressing anger in "action on behalf
of justice and participation in the transformation of the world."[30]
For those involved in ministry, education for justice and peace will
be among the primary means.[31]

---

29. Cf. *Summa Theologica I-II.* 46.2, 4, 6.
30. Synod of Bishops, 1971, *Justice in the World*, in *Acta Apostolicae Sedis* 63 (1971)
    924.
31. Cf. John Paul II, "Women: Teachers of Peace," *Origins* 24 (#28; December 22,
    1994) 465-69; Jorge Mejia, "Dimensions of the Bishop's Essential Ministry of
    Peace," *Origins* 24 (#39; March 16, 1995) 641-48; Dolores Leckey, "Peacemaking
    and Creativity: Three Dynamics," *Origins* 24 (#45; April 27, 1995) 777-80.
    Leckey focuses on three dynamics that make for peace: listening, beauty, and
    laughter.

Reconciliation too will be one of the basic goals of ministry. I am reminded of the role that the Community of Sant'Egidio played in mediating the peace in Mozambique. After fifteen years of civil war, "human wisdom" would surely have doubted the ability of a "powerless" Italian community to accomplish what other much more "powerful" agencies had failed to do. Yet the negotiations were successfully completed in 1992 and peace continues to reign in that country. Could not other groups have similar courage in offering their services as ministers of reconciliation?

Conversation and dialogue will, in the lives of the gentle, be the primary means for settling conflicts, accompanied by suffering love. These are the tools that Jesus himself used; he himself is "our peace, and breaks down the wall of separation" (Eph 2:14). If the community of his disciples has a genuine passion for dialogue, justice, and peace, then it is a clear sign that the kingdom of God is at hand.

"Passionate" gentleness[32] knows how to direct anger to root out injustice, to channel it so that "justice rolls like a river" (Am 5:24). W. E. B. DuBois sums up this gentle passion in a lovely prayer:

> Give us grace, O God, to dare to do the deed which we well know cries to be done. Let us not hesitate because of ease, or the words of men's mouths, or our own lives. Mighty causes are calling us — the freeing of women, the training of children, the putting down of hate and murder and poverty — all these and more. But they call with voices that mean work and sacrifice and death. Mercifully, grant us, O God, the spirit of Esther, that we say: I will go unto the King and if I perish, I perish. Amen.[33]

---

32. Cf. Walter Burghardt, "A Faith That Does Justice," Warren Series Lectures, in *Catholic Studies* (#18; November 17, 1991) 9.
33. David Levering Lewis, ed., *W.E.B. DuBois: A Reader* (1995).

A Time for Distinguishing

Some Helpful Distinctions in Catholic Life[1]

On the surface, distinctions seem to divide. As you begin to distinguish the personalities of identical twins, for example, you know them little by little as separate individuals. They are no longer an undefined, confused unity, but two independent persons.

Distinctions, however, are actually a tool in uniting. They enable us to view different aspects of reality within the context of a larger truth. They draw us toward the unifying source that grounds all reality—truth, being, God.

I offer below some distinctions that are helpful for living peacefully as a Catholic. They flow from my own experience and that of others. I write from the perspective of a Superior General of an apostolic society, but I sense that they may be of use to all Catholics. I hope that they will enable the reader to "distinguish in order to unite" as the original title of Jacques Maritain's classical work, *The Degrees of Knowledge*,[2] put it.

Distinguishing the Church from the hierarchy

Once, at table in London, I happened to be discussing the movie, "Mission," with a priest who had liked it very much. He asked me what my own reaction had been. I said that I liked it too, but that it certainly painted a bleak picture of the Church. He replied, quite spontaneously, that he thought it had presented an exciting, positive picture of the Church. Immediately I realized that I had fallen into the trap of identifying the Church with the hierarchy (which, in "Mission," performed rather badly!).

The Church is the people of God, the body of Christ, the community of disciples gathered together by the word of the Lord and nourished by sacramental signs of his presence. Within that context, the hierarchy plays an important role of leadership. It has

---

1. Article originally published in *America*, October 14, 1995.
2. Jacques Maritain, *The Degrees of Knowledge* (London, 1937).

a special ministry in confirming our faith, in challenging us to conversion, in organizing other ministries within the Christian community. But, it is one ministry among many others, even if a very basic one. The life of the Church throbs in the hearts of all believers, especially in the most humble, the most abandoned, the poor. Saint Vincent de Paul used to say: "The poor have the true religion" (SV XI, 201). It is important, while giving the hierarchy its due place, not to exaggerate its role. Basically, it serves the Church. At times when there are tensions between some Church members and the hierarchy or scandals within the hierarchy itself, it is useful to note that the Church is thriving at its roots in the lives of the poor.

Distinguishing morality from legality

This is a classical distinction that most of us know in theory but that we easily forget in practice.

Morality involves the rightness and wrongness of human acts. In Catholic moral theology, the human person is the criterion for what is morally right and wrong.[3] The human conscience, if well-formed, arrives at moral decisions by judging their effect on the human person, integrally considered. The fundamental moral stance of an individual flows from the choices he or she makes. Through individual choices a person, often gradually, makes a basic choice with respect to the whole direction of his or her life. In doing so, individuals accept or reject, deep down within their own persons, God's enabling love.

Legality refers to whether an action is permitted by civil law or not. Something is illegal when it is prohibited by the law. Something is legal when it is permitted (either because the law says so explicitly or because the law is silent). There are many "legal" actions that are quite immoral. A husband who lies to his wife about where he was last night commits an immoral action, but it is quite legal to do so. Consenting adults who have casual sex or who are involved in aborting a child they find inconvenient surely act against the good of the human person, but they violate no civil law. In matters of

---

3. *Gaudium et Spes* 51.

justice and human rights too, it is often possible to act quite legally, even though one's actions may ultimately be harmful to the poor.

On the other hand, there are illegal acts which can be quite moral. The Church has a long tradition of recognizing these, from the time of the Acts of the Apostles: "Better to obey God than men!" (Acts 4:19).

Distinguishing holiness from piety

Holiness is immersion in God. In the saints it takes a variety of forms: active, contemplative, mixed. Different saints often focus on varied aspects of the gospels. As a result, the Church's holiness shines forth in wonderfully varied colors. Dedication to the truth, active service of the most needy, renunciation for the sake of the Lord and the gospel, deep faithful commitment to prayer, laying down one's life for one's friends are all classical forms that holiness has taken. As is evident, holiness often has a very explicit evangelical foundation; at other times, its manifestations can be rather anonymously Christian, while nonetheless heroic.

Piety, at least in common parlance, means a commitment to certain spiritual exercises and practices. Pious exercises are clearly intended as means toward growth in holiness, but unfortunately, for a variety of reasons, they do not always achieve their purpose. I have known people who were quite "pious," who never missed prayer, but were dreadful to live with in community. Frequently people, after describing how bizarre or difficult someone is, conclude their discourse by saying, "but he's a holy man." This is, it seems to me, the fatal error of failing to distinguish between holiness and piety. When this error is made, one is tempted to say: "If that's holiness, leave me out!"

Distinguishing perfection from not making mistakes

Over the years, I have worked with a number of people, some of them superiors, who were very cautious about making mistakes. In fact, they were so "prudent" that they rarely made any.

But they also rarely risked anything. If one thinks of being perfect as making no errors, then life is likely to be filled with caution, the "tried and true," the safe. If one thinks of perfection in its root sense (*per* + *ficere*) as doing things thoroughly, then one must often try various alternatives, recognizing that one will make mistakes. There are acceptable risks that bear with them the possibility of failure, but also bear the possibility of very significant fruit.

Distinguishing holiness from sinlessness

Teresa of Avila once said that when she lived quietly in the cloister she committed very few sins, but when she became an active founder and visitor of monasteries she sinned much more frequently, but grew much more in charity.

To put it paradoxically, some of the great saints have been notable sinners. The New Testament attests to this in its accounts about Peter. The list of saints whose failings are very evident is quite long (the apostles, Augustine, Jerome, to name just a few).

One might think, erroneously, that all of these underwent a striking conversion and then remained more or less "sinless" afterwards. But that is not at all the case. The saints struggle with their sinfulness right to the end. In fact, those who speak on the matter usually attest that they grow more and more aware of their sinfulness, even as they grow more conscious of the loving forgiveness of God. A person is not holy because he or she is sinless. A person is holy because he allows God, with utter confidence, to forgive his sins, to take hold of his life, and to use it as he wills.

Distinguishing the good from the difficult

There is a Pelagian strain that asserts itself, from time to time, in the lives of all, particularly among virtuous people. It identifies the good with the difficult. Of course, the good and the difficult are sometimes quite identical in the concrete. One may have to work hard to achieve good. One may have to sacrifice. One may have to suffer and forgive.

But sometimes the good is very pleasurable. It is good to have fun, to celebrate, to rejoice. It is good to love and to be loved. It is good to know peace.

In fact, the first three fruits of the Spirit are love, joy, peace. All are very enjoyable!

Distinguishing rest from self-indulgence

Rest is important. It is an essential part of a balanced lifestyle. In fact, the Lord *commands* rest on the Sabbath and on great feasts (Ex 20:8ff). Rest is also a sign of trust in the Lord. "Unless the Lord builds the house, they labor in vain who build it. Unless the Lord guards the city, in vain does the guard keep watch" (Ps 127:2). One of the treasured Christian images for life after death is "rest."

In the Aristotelian tradition, leisure stands among the highest forms of human activity. In fact, for Aristotle, the human person works in order to have leisure (whereas we tend to say that we rest so that we can work better!).

Self-indulgence is quite another matter. It means that one goes beyond the bounds of what is helpful for human growth. It means that one's quest for pleasure (which could take the form of rest too) impedes the person from realizing more important human goals (like spiritual, intellectual, moral, cultural growth; or the activities that are essential in relationships with others, like work, time together, listening, etc.).

Self-indulgence isolates us by nourishing egotism. Leisure, on the other hand, liberates us for higher values.

Distinguishing humility from passivity

Humility is a basic evangelical virtue by which we recognize everything as God's gift and ourselves as completely dependent upon him. The humble acknowledge their limits as creatures and their interdependence with others. They also recognize their sinfulness and their need for God's redeeming love, while trusting that God forgives abundantly. In Luke's gospel, Mary is the paradigm of humility. She knows that God "who is mighty has done great things for me and holy is his name" (Lk 1:49).

But the humble need by no means be passive. In fact, they have exuberant confidence in the power of God. When necessary, they speak fearlessly, knowing that God is with them. They are willing to undertake difficult, even daunting projects because they believe, like Abraham, that God can raise even the dead to life (Heb 11:19).

Distinguishing obedience to authority from obedience to monarchy

Occasionally some make the error of thinking that obedience is more perfect if the system imposing it is monarchical. In fact, I have known superiors who felt that democratic structures detracted significantly from the value of obedience.

But that is not necessarily true at all. Obedience, like most significant Christian values, is not restricted to any particular type of governmental system or cultural context (though the temptation for those living in a particular culture may be to think that it is). The Church, in fact, has a long tradition of democratic structures for deciding some very important issues (the election of a pope, the enacting of documents during general councils, the elections of abbots, at various times in history the election of bishops, etc.). The demands of obedience afterwards are quite real in those settings too.

Democratic processes can result in decisions that are quite binding and that make difficult demands. At a general chapter, for example, a democratic system is used for electing a superior general and for composing constitutions and statutes. Afterwards, all the members are then bound to obey the General and live by the constitutions. The asceticism of obedience surely makes difficult demands on those who voted for another candidate or for a different version of the constitutions (or even *against* the accepted version). In fact, obedience, in this same context, can make painful demands on everyone, since faithful observance and generous response to leadership require follow-through and constancy.

Distinguishing criticism from disloyalty

Many of us in authority get thin-skinned about criticism. We think of our critics as disloyal. But this is not necessarily true. A thoughtful critic may be among society's most faithful members.

Socrates maintained to his death that he was Athens' most loyal citizen.

A frivolous critic may surely be disloyal, since he or she shows little attachment either to individuals or to the group. But a thoughtful critic is a friend. It is helpful for those of us in authority if we can accept disagreement, criticism, and dissent as facts of life. Even more, it is crucial that we listen to dissenting voices in order to weigh carefully what they are saying.

Dissent within the Church has pastoral and doctrinal limits. Pastorally, one must judge whether the time and circumstances are ripe for voicing disagreement. Doctrinally, one must weigh the force with which a teaching is proposed by the Church and its place within the hierarchy of truths. Within that framework, dissent can play a very healthy role in the life of the Church.

Distinctions often help us avoid unnecessary problems. By enabling us to sort out various realities and situate them in a larger context, they give us a clearer view of the truth. In that sense, they are ultimately liberating, since they move us from confusion toward clarity.

A Time for Making Friends

Hoops of Steel
Some Reflections on Friendship

Friendship lies more in the living than in the explaining. Faithful friends often say little about their relationship. They grasp intuitively that it exists. I know someone who almost never speaks of his relationship with God but who, I am certain, is God's intimate friend. I also know of human friendships that are long-lived, faithful, and utterly spontaneous, without any felt need for analysis or for professing "perpetual amity."

So I hesitate to write about friendship. It is, moreover, one of those many-faceted, all-embracing topics that touches on the transcendent and the imminent, the vertical and the horizontal. We can speak of the whole story of God's relationship with us in terms of friendship: creation and redemption, grace and sin, salvation and eternal life. Even to write only of human friendship is a daunting undertaking, since it is multi-leveled and varied, with a perennial fascination about it that has drawn philosophers and theologians to analyze it in detail.

Still I write, prompted by a wiser older friend, who insists on the importance of the topic for today. I share his conviction. Friends are crucial on life's journey. I have often been struck by Polonius' advice to his son in *Hamlet*:

> *The friends thou hast, and their adoption tried,*
> *Grapple them to thy soul with hoops of steel.*[1]

In this chapter I offer some reflections on friendship "yesterday and today," so to speak.

---

1. William Shakespeare, *Hamlet*, Act I, Scene 3.

Friendship in the Writings of Vincent De Paul

Saint Vincent did not write systematically about friendship. In fact, he wrote very little about it, and usually only in passing. Some of his longest treatments of the subject come in a somewhat negative context when he warns the members of his family about the dangers of its excesses.

There is little doubt, however, that Vincent viewed friendship quite positively. It is, in fact, a key concept for him when speaking about community. He urges the members of the Congregation of the Mission to live together *in morem tamen carorum amicorum*, which we might translate "like dear friends" or "like friends who love one another" (CR VIII, 2). He states that friendship is a gift from God (SV IV, 583; V, 64). He tells Sr. Charlotte Royer that it is the source of union and peace (SV VI, 46). In a conference given to the Daughters of Charity on May 30, 1658, he urges the members of the community to have the forbearance and respect that are the foundation of genuine friendship so that they can create a "paradise even in this world" (SV X, 478). His talks make it clear that humility, gentleness, mutual respect, simplicity, cordiality, and acceptance of one another's faults are all very helpful for building up the healthy friendships that bind communities together.

But the same paragraph of the *Common Rules* of the Vincentians that describes friendship so positively also adds a cautionary note to which Vincent often returns: "They shall avoid particular friendships" (CR VIII, 2).[2] He states that such friendships are "the origin of divisions and the ruin of Congregations" (CR VIII, 2). The Rules of the Daughters of Charity contain a similar caution: "Although the Sisters ought to love one another deeply, they shall, nonetheless, be very careful about particular friendships."[3]

Saint Vincent takes up this topic in detail while speaking with the Daughters of Charity about the virtue of cordiality. He describes

---

2. Saint Vincent is by no means unique in his preoccupation with particular friendship. There is a long history of writing on the subject in the monastic tradition. Well over a thousand years earlier than Vincent, John Cassian was writing about particular friendships in his *Institutions* (Book 2, chap. 15).

3. *Common Rules of the Daughters of Charity*, 40 (in the version used by Saint Vincent) or Chapter VI, # 1 in the version prepared by René Alméras.

particular friendships as an excess of this virtue (whereas the defect of the same virtue is coldness, distance, and the failure to show any signs of friendship). He notes that particular friendships lead to many evils within the community: little intrigues, gossip, murmuring, disobedience, division in a house (SV X, 494-96). He uses some very strong language in talking about this problem. Particular friendships are a "plague" (SV XI, 103), the "ruin" (SV XIII, 556) of community. They are "animal love," like that of a "horse or an ass" (SV X, 496), rather than "Christian love." There are implicit, and sometimes explicit sexual overtones in this discussion. Vincent notes that while particular friendships are dangerous among the members of the community, they are even more so when formed with people outside the Company, especially with those of the opposite sex (SV X, 488). Still, even in a context where he speaks with such caution, he is confident that the Daughters of Charity will "excel in love of the neighbor, particularly their own companions" (SV XIII, 556, 564).

As is evident from what has been stated above, Vincent's treatment of friendship is not very extensive. On the one hand he esteems it highly; on the other hand he speaks of it rather cautiously.[4] Beyond that, he says very little explicitly. One might, from the overall context of his life and writings, deduce further conclusions about "friendship with God" and "friendship with the poor," but actually Vincent says very little directly about such matters.

Saint Vincent's Practice of Friendship

We often learn much more from what people do than from what they say. Consequently, especially since Saint Vincent said so little about friendship, it is very useful for us to examine his relationships. He had many friends: male and female, clerical and lay, rich and poor.

---

4. To broaden the context, it may be helpful to note that Vincent's friend, Francis de Sales, wrote even more cautiously: "Friendship is the most dangerous of all types of love." Cf. *Introduction to a Devout Life*, translated by John Ryan (New York: Doubleday, 1989), Part III, 17, p. 169. It is clear that Vincent borrows abundantly from Francis' treatment of friendship.

His spiritual guides

Other writers have already described in detail Vincent's relationship with his spiritual directors.[5] It is very clear that he owed much to masters like Pierre de Bérulle, André Duval, and Francis de Sales, who were all very influential "soul friends."

Echoing his own experience, Vincent often spoke of the need for good spiritual direction (SV XII, 451-85; XIII, 142). He wrote to Jeanne Lepeintre on February 23, 1650: "Spiritual direction is very useful. It is a source of advice when in difficulties, of help when discouraged, of safety when tempted, and of strength when overwhelmed. Finally, it is source of benefit and consolation when the director is really charitable, prudent, and experienced" (SV III, 614). His own relationship with his "soul friends" surely had a very positive impact on his life.

Pierre de Bérulle (1575-1629) had a profound impact on Vincent's spirituality, helping him develop a deeply christological worldview and a keen interest in the reform of the clergy. Bérulle is often regarded as the principal figure in the "French School"[6] of spirituality, though Vincent is not usually considered a member of this school. A prolific writer, Bérulle was very much involved in the political and ecclesiastical life of his time and made abundant friends and enemies. Saint Vincent came into contact with him in 1610 and years later spoke of him as "one of the holiest persons whom I have met" (SV XI, 139). Though Bérulle had an abiding influence on Vincent, the disciple always maintained considerable independence from his teacher. In that sense, Bérulle was only one of several great "soul friends" in Saint Vincent's life. Their contact lasted seven or eight years. Then they went decidedly separate ways. While Saint Vincent consistently spoke very positively of Bérulle in public, even after the parting of their ways, nonetheless it is evident that they differed considerably on the level of practical judgment. Though the

---

5. Cf. Luigi Mezzadri and Luigi Nuovo, "The Directors of Saint Vincent," *Vincentian Heritage* VI (#2; 1985) 173-79.
6. Cf. Raymond Deville, *L'École française de spiritualité* (Paris: Desclée, 1987). Also, *Bérulle and the French School*, edited with an introduction by William M. Thompson (New York: Paulist, 1989).

details are not clear, the rupture in their relationship probably took place around 1618 when Bérulle was attempting to impose upon the Carmelites a fourth vow of "slavery" to Christ and the Blessed Virgin.[7] This produced a bitter row in which he lost some of his closest friends, among them André Duval and Madame Acarie. It seems likely that also Vincent de Paul on this occasion decided that he had had enough of the intrigues of the Bérullian world.

Vincent's second great soul friend was "the good Monsieur Duval" (SV XII, 100, 376), for whom he had enormous respect throughout his life. André Duval (1564-1638) was a much more realistic, moderate, concrete director. Saint Vincent said of him that he "was a great doctor of the Sorbonne but was greater still by the holiness of his life" (SV XI, 154). He had a strong loyalty to the Holy See and wrote a treatise on the authority of the Roman Pontiff. He was also one of the closest friends of Madame Acarie and composed her biography shortly after her death. Until the time of his death in 1638, he served as Saint Vincent's counselor. His nephew,[8] Robert Duval, who wrote his life, states:

> Vincent de Paul, Founder and Superior General of the Priests of the Mission, humbly said on different occasions that the origin and founding of his Company were due in great part to the Venerable André. . . . He (Vincent) undertook nothing without his advice. In the same way he wished that his companions appeal to him for the solution of the difficult cases which were presented during the missions. Our Doctor always responded quickly and with precision to these requests, with the result that the Priests of the Mission have collected the majority of them so that they might be used on similar occasions.[9]

Vincent had a portrait of Duval hung at St. Lazare.[10] He told others: "Everything is holy in M. Duval. If I wanted to list all the virtues that I have seen in him I would never finish. So I have reached

---

7. José María Román, *San Vicente de Paúl, Biografía* (Madrid: BAC, 1981) I, 101.

8. Two other nephews of his were prominent Vincentians, Jean and Philippe Le Vacher.

9. Robert Duval, *La Vie du Maître André Duval* (Versailles: Bibliothèque Municipale) 72-75.

10. *Ibid.*, 295.

the conclusion that I have seen nothing in him that did not appear to me holy."[11]

The third great spiritual teacher of Vincent de Paul was Francis de Sales (1567-1622). A model bishop, large-hearted and full of tenderness, Francis had a great interest in lay spirituality and knew how to explain the mystery of holiness in terms that were concrete and practical. Vincent borrowed many ideas from Francis' *Introduction to a Devout Life* and *Treatise on the Love of God*, but he learned even more from the man himself, making his own Francis' gentleness and effective love. Vincent also came to comprehend Francis' unsuccessful efforts to establish a community of Sisters not bound by the cloister. Knowledge of this experience was undoubtedly very helpful to him in his own foundation of the Daughters of Charity.

Their relationship was relatively short-lived since Vincent came to know Francis only around 1618 when the latter came to Paris to help negotiate the marriage of the Prince of Piedmont with Christina of France, the sister of Louis XIII. Despite huge differences in background, they quickly became friends, communicating easily and with great familiarity (SV XIII, 67-69). The impression of Francis' holiness remained imprinted in Vincent's heart and memory. He had Francis' portrait placed in the conference room at St. Lazare and when speaking with both the Vincentians and the Daughters of Charity referred to him as "our blessed father" (SV II, 70, 212). They had rather frequent contact during Francis' stay in Paris, which lasted about a year, but it is not clear how much contact they had beyond that. Francis died in 1622, having commended the care of the Visitation Sisters to Vincent, a sign of the great respect that this upper class bishop had for this younger priest of peasant background. Vincent testified enthusiastically at the cause of Francis' beatification and frequently referred to him and his writings throughout his life.

It is perhaps worth noting that all three of these "soul friends" of Vincent de Paul were enthusiastic admirers of the remarkable Madame Acarie and frequented her salon. Benedict of Canfield too, who also had a considerable influence on Vincent's spirituality, was

---

11. *Ibid.*, 411.

part of the circle of "la belle Acarie."[12] This leads one to ask whether Vincent himself, as a young priest, might have known this extraordinary woman, mother of six children, who had such an enormous impact on so many of the religious leaders of his day that some regard her as the most influential spiritual leader of her time.

Three Very Close Friends

It is not easy to choose among Vincent's other friends. Over his long life he had many. In making a choice, one hesitates to leave out "the incomparable M. Lambert" aux Couteaux (SV IV, 567), in whom Vincent had such confidence that he wrote to Bishop Ingoli: "I must admit, Your Excellency, that the loss of this man is like having me tear out one of my eyes or cut off one of my arms."[13]

One might be eager to mention Jane Frances de Chantal, whose relationship with Vincent was one that combined both great respect and tenderness. Vincent addresses Jane Frances as someone who is "so much our honored Mother that she is mine alone and whom I honor and cherish more tenderly than any child ever honored and loved its mother since our Lord; and it seems to me that I do so to such an extent that I have sufficient esteem and love to be able to share it with the whole world; and that, in truth, without exaggeration" (SV II, 86-87).

Louis de Chandenier, who "lived like a saint and died like a missionary" (SV VIII, 302), also draws one's attention in compiling a list of friends. Vincent, on hearing the news of his death, broke into tears (something which is recorded on no other occasion in his life).

Abelly reminds us that Charles du Fresne, Sieur de Villeneuve, was one of Vincent's closest friends, "the person to whom I have the greatest obligation and desire to obey in this world."[14]

The irrepressible Madame Goussault also comes to mind. She was Vincent's ebullient companion in so many enterprises, including

---

12. Cf. Deville, *L'École française*, 24. Cf., also, Bruno de Jésus-Marie, *La Belle Acarie* (Paris, 1942).
13. SV I, 208; cf. *Notices sur les prêtres, clercs et frères défunts de la Congrégation de la Mission* (Paris: Pillet et Dumoulin, 1885), first series, vol. II, pages 1-28.
14. SV III, 276; cf. SV I, 23 and Abelly, Book I, 21.

some of the original foundations of the Daughters of Charity and the early formation of the sisters.[15] She had a contagious joy which Vincent urged Louise de Marillac to share in (SV I, 502). He often recalled her peaceful death after a long painful sickness. She died "with joy and jubilation," he told Louis Lebreton (SV I, 595; cf. SV XIII, 781).

Likewise, one cannot forget Jean Duverger de Hauranne, the Abbé de Saint-Cyran, "one of the best men I have ever seen" (SV XIII, 87). This important figure in the history of Jansenism was Vincent's intimate friend from 1622 to 1643. Though a number of the saint's biographers have attempted to downplay, for political and hagiographical reasons, their closeness, it is evident that they were the best of friends. For years, they shared a common purse and many common concerns. Even after Vincent became a formidable adversary of Jansenism, it is remarkable how discreetly he spoke about his friend. He gave a long deposition in favor of Saint-Cyran on March 31 to April 2, 1639. At some risk to his own reputation, he went, upon Saint-Cyran's death, to pray in the chapel where his friend's body lay.

But, since I must choose, let me dwell for a moment on three of the closest friends of Vincent de Paul.

Louise de Marillac (1591-1660)

Vincent's relationship with Louise was a rocky one at the start. She felt a certain repugnance for entering into spiritual direction with someone who was so very different in background from the distinguished Msgr. Camus, Bishop of Belley, her former director.[16] Vincent too hesitated. Some of the early letters between them are quite formal. At times too Vincent's responses are rather brusque. One need only recall, in this regard, the rather harried letter that Louise wrote to Vincent on a Tuesday evening around June 1642, with nineteen questions. On it, Vincent wrote a reply in his own hand: "I will try to be there in the late afternoon. However, let me tell you that you are a woman of little faith and I am your servant"

15. Madame Goussault was also the aunt of Vincent's successor, René Alméras.
16. Msgr. Camus was also a nephew of Louise's stepmother.

(SW 73). But a remarkable friendship grew up between the two of them. It would be a mistake to think that their relationship was "all business." They related with warmth and affection, without, as Vincent might put it, "the slightest suspicion of unchastity" (CR IV, 1).

Their letters contain some lovely passages filled with human tenderness. In October 1627, Vincent tells Louise de Marillac: "I am writing to you at about midnight and am a little tired. Forgive my heart if it is not a little more expansive in this letter. Be faithful to your faithful lover who is our Lord. Also be very simple and humble. And I shall be in the love of our Lord and his holy mother . . . " (SV I, 30). On New Year's Day 1638, he concludes his letter to her: "I wish you a young heart and a love in its first bloom for him who loves us unceasingly and as tenderly as if he were just beginning to love us. For all God's pleasures are ever new and full of variety, although he never changes. I am in his love, with an affection such as his goodness desires and which I owe him out of love for him, Mademoiselle, your most humble servant . . . " (SV I, 417-18). In another letter he remarks, both tenderly and teasingly: "I am not asking you to remember me in your prayers, because I have no doubt that, after little Le Gras (her troubled son), you put me in first place" (SV I, 384).

Vincent and Louise shared enormous undertakings over the thirty-five years of their relationship. Together they laid the foundations for the Company of the Daughters of Charity and guided the early years of its growth. Louise walked with the Sisters step by step, teaching them God's ways and carefully organizing their life and work. Vincent accompanied her on her spiritual journey, sometimes with a strong hand during her earlier anxious years. With the passage of time they came to a remarkable understanding of one another, each recognizing the other's strengths and weaknesses and each promoting the other's gifts.[17]

The correspondence of their final years, when both were sick, is quite touching, as they exchange remedies for their illnesses and

---

17. Cf. "Vincent de Paul—Louise de Marillac: Une Veritable Amitié" in Elisabeth Charpy, *Contre Vents et Marées, Louise de Marillac* (Paris: Compagnie des Filles de la Charité, 1988) 149-65.

express their thoughts and feelings with great simplicity. Just a short time before her own death, Louise writes to Vincent:

> For the love of God, allow me to ask for news of your health. Is the swelling in your legs increasing? Are you in less pain? Do you have any traces of fever? With the openness of a daughter toward her Most Honored Father, I cannot refrain from saying that I believe that it is absolutely essential for you to be purged thoroughly but gently to make up for the inadequacy of nature, which interferes with sweating, because it is also very dangerous to induce a sweat by artificial means.
>
> As a sick person, you must take some nourishment in the evening, but not bread or wine. Herbs have an unpleasant taste, but they build good blood. Cornachin powder—eighteen or twenty-one grains only—is very good occasionally for children or old people. It does not upset the system and it draws off fluids without leaving the body dehydrated. Because I am well acquainted with this remedy, I dare to suggest it. I know that you will not use it without consultation.
>
> I would truly like to know how you really are. (SW, 670-71)

These two wonderful friends died within six months of one another. Only a month before Louise's death, a second great friend of Vincent's went to God, Monsieur Portail.

Antoine Portail (1590-1660)

Antoine Portail was, along with Vincent de Paul, François Du Coudray, and Jean de la Salle, one of the original members of the Congregation of the Mission. He and Vincent first became acquainted at Clichy in 1612 while Portail was studying at the Sorbonne. During Vincent's second period with the de Gondi's, it was Portail who did most of the tutoring of the children since Vincent was busy with other matters. He remained Vincent's faithful companion and collaborator throughout life, from the time of his ordination in 1622 until his death, which took place only seven months before that of the founder. Vincent first engaged him in the service of the galley slaves and then initiated him into the ministry of the missions and the work with the ordinands. After 1640, he was the first director of the Daughters of Charity. He played a great role in their formation, participating frequently at their conferences on spiritual topics. In 1642 he became Saint Vincent's first assistant in the government of the growing Congregation of the Mission.

In some ways Portail was Saint Vincent's eyes and ears, visiting the houses of both the Congregation of the Mission and the Daughters of Charity (SV I, 43, n. 3). He was his confidant and counselor. Vincent said publicly that Portail "always put up with my weaknesses" (SV XII, 12). Portail was very shy, hesitating for years to enter the pulpit and doing so only in 1630, almost twenty years after he had begun to collaborate with Vincent. He must have overcome his shyness to a considerable extent since Vincent later extols him as a model of simplicity in preaching (SV XI, 275, 283). He made long visitations in France and Italy. On one tour of visitations he left Paris in 1646, going to the west of France; he then went south, crossed into Italy, and did not return to St. Lazare until September 1649.

It was to Portail that Vincent wrote one of his best remembered exhortations:

> Remember, Father, we live in Jesus Christ through the death of Jesus Christ, and we must die in Jesus Christ through the life of Jesus Christ, and our life must be hidden in Jesus Christ and filled with Jesus Christ, and in order to die as Jesus Christ, we must live as Jesus Christ. (SV I, 295)

Bertrand Ducournau (1614-1677)

Ducournau was thirty years of age when he met Vincent de Paul in 1644. He was a shrewd, enterprising young man who first worked for a notary and then as a secretary for one of the principal persons of Bayonne. He acquired a reputation as an expert in calligraphy and was invited by the new Bishop of Bayonne, François Fouquet, to help at the episcopal palace. Disappointed with his job there, he went to Paris where he took up a new job as secretary to a Viceroy, Urbain de Maillé.

Engaged to be married, but struggling with thoughts about entering some form of community life, he went to St. Lazare to make a retreat, having agreed to meet a friend there. The friend failed to show up, but Bertrand made the retreat and, after a conversation with Vincent de Paul, decided to enter the Congregation of the Mission as a brother. After he took vows, his superiors, aware of his beautiful handwriting, asked him to assist Vincent, whose new work on the Council of Conscience meant that his correspondence was piling up more and more. The first letter written in Ducournau's hand was that of May 3, 1645.

From that time on, Bertrand was almost always at Saint Vincent's side. He handled much of the daily mail and often accompanied Vincent on very important business matters. He went along on the difficult journey in 1649 that took Vincent to the residence of Anne of Austria to ask the queen to remove Mazarin from the government. He was one of the few who witnessed Vincent's painful disappointment on that occasion. He was often an intermediary between Vincent and others, carrying messages back and forth. At times he substituted for him at meetings. He stood by Vincent faithfully during the years of his sickness and death. Br. Pierre Chollier, Ducournau's assistant in the secretariat, wrote of Bertrand: "Monsieur Vincent loved him, cherished him, and esteemed him, since he made him the recipient of even the most secret matters."[18] Ducournau is one of the most important figures in preserving the "Vincentian tradition," since he helped organize several "conspiracies," behind Vincent's back, to preserve his writings and his words.

Vincent and Ducournau were both from the same part of the country, the latter coming from Amou, not far from Dax. One can imagine them speaking intimately in French, with the same accent, exchanging thoughts about the confidential affairs of the Congregation.

Reviewing all these friendships at a distance of more than three centuries, it is difficult to assess them, for a variety of reasons. First, we possess only about ten percent of Vincent's correspondence; the rest is lost to us, much of it forever. Secondly, even in the letters that we do have, the language is often stylized, formal, and somewhat flowery, as is evident, for example, in the correspondence with Jane de Chantal and Louise de Marillac. Expressions of warmth and affection are very much colored by the piety of the time. Thirdly, in

18. *Notices* I, 377f.

much of the correspondence (and, in fact, in most of his relationships over the last thirty-five years of his life), Vincent is the superior or the spiritual guide of the persons to whom he is writing. They are not peers, so to speak. While friendship does not always demand that the parties be precisely "equals," it does demand a certain equality, with free give-and-take. This free, back-and-forth kind of relationship might not easily have been possible between Vincent and most of his colleagues, especially in the last three decades of his life. He was quickly becoming a revered figure, the founder of two Communities, a member of the king's Council of Conscience, and one of the most sought-after persons of the day.

A Horizon Shift Between the Seventeenth and the Twentieth Centuries

In a number of earlier essays I have described the notion of horizon shifts and their influence on how we perceive reality.[19] Horizon shifts,[20] whether we react favorably or unfavorably to them, inevitably affect the way we view life (Rome as viewed from the top of St. Peter's looks very different from Rome as seen from inside a crowded bus!). Over the last several years I have written about various horizon shifts that have taken place between the seventeenth and twentieth centuries which have ramifications for the way we interpret Saint Vincent's teaching today.

Here, let me mention a further, very important change in perspective, related to several of those alluded to above, which affects the way we think and talk about friendship: a shift from focusing on the human person primarily as an individual to viewing the person as essentially social.

---

19. Cf. Robert Maloney, "The Four Vincentian Vows: Yesterday and Today" in *The Way of Vincent de Paul* (Brooklyn: New City Press, 1992) 90-96; "Five Characteristic Virtues: Yesterday and Today" in *ibid.*, 48-52; Providence Revisited" in *He Hears the Cry of the Poor* (Hyde Park, New York: New City Press, 1995) 60-63; "Mental Prayer, Yesterday and Today: The Vincentian Tradition" in *ibid.*, 83-85.
20. Cf. Thomas Kuhn, *The Structure of Scientific Revolutions* (Chicago: University of Chicago Press, 1962). This well-known thinker, whose writings on horizon shifts have been so influential, died recently, I am sad to say.

Since Saint Vincent's time, and especially over the last hundred years, there has been an increasing emphasis on human relationships and on the social dimension of the human person. This shift is quite evident in theory, even if it is not consistently realized in practice. A long line of encyclicals and other official Church documents has placed the social aspect of the human person in the forefront of Catholic theological consciousness. In this regard, one need only recall *Rerum Novarum* (1891), *Quadragesimo Anno* (1931), *Pacem in Terris* (1963), *Gaudium et Spes* (1965), *Populorum Progressio* (1967), *Octogesima Adveniens* (1971), *Justice in the World* (1971), *Redemptor Hominis* (1979), *Laborem Exercens* (1981), *Sollicitudo Rei Socialis* (1987), *Centesimus Annus* (1991).[21]

Contemporary philosophy has also had an enormous influence on popular thinking. Martin Buber has made the "I-Thou" relationship a familiar concept for modern students.[22] Popularized books on psychology have used "interpersonal" philosophical underpinnings to support transactional theories and self-help practices.[23] In this perspective, the place of intimate friends becomes extremely important. In fact, recent statistics indicate that the primary characteristic energizing young people today is their "search for relationships, friendship and community."[24]

Beyond the interpersonal thrust of the "I-Thou," the 20th century has seen an increasingly broader emphasis on the social (the wider circle of relationships a person has) and the societal (broader still than one's social circle of friends and extending to groups, states, nations), with a growing consciousness of the interrelatedness of all human persons and of all created reality (including contemporary ecological concerns).[25]

While it is evident that one cannot be "friends" with everybody,

---

21. Cf. United States Catholic Conference, "A Century of Social Teaching" (Washington: USCC Publishing Services, 1990) 4-7. Cf. also, a very interesting article by Walter Burghardt, "Characteristics of Social Justice Spirituality," *Origins* 24 (#9, July 21, 1994) 157-64.

22. Cf. M. Buber, *The Way of Man According to the Teaching of Hasidism* (Secaucus: Citadel, 1966).

23. Cf. Thomas Harris, *I'm OK, You're OK* (New York: Avon, 1973), which had an immense popularity.

24. Cf. *Origins* 25 (#31; January 25, 1996) 514.

25. Cf. *Sollicitudo Rei Socialis* 26.

this horizon shift makes it clear that we can be fully human only when we establish healthy, responsible, lasting bonds with others on many different levels. The human person is ultimately a "person-in-relation."

Having stated the importance of this horizon shift in theory, let me quickly add that there are many opposite tendencies in practice. Numerous contemporary authors point out that within American society in particular, as well as in other parts of the world, there is an exaggerated individualism that at times exalts one's own personal freedom at the expense of the freedom of others and that in the long run has serious negative consequences for the well-being of society.[26] Naturally, excessive individualism has serious ramifications for friendship and community life as well.[27] As Margaret Miles recently put it: "Modern rhetoric about the high value of friendship frequently conceals the fundamental narcissistic isolation of some twentieth-century people."[28]

Some Reflections on Friendship Today

Given the horizon shift described above, today we tend to focus more on our mutual interdependence than would have been the case in the time of Saint Vincent. We recognize, at least in theory, that what one person does inevitably affects others, for good or for bad. Within that context, we see friendships as having an essential role in healthy, human growth. In formation, for example, it is a good sign when a candidate has close friends and a very bad sign when he or she has none. It is clear that friendship—this deeply appreciated, complex reality—rates very high on the list of human values today. Below I offer a few reflections on some of its facets.

---

26. Cf. Robert Bellah, et. al., *Habits of the Heart* (New York: Harper & Row, 1985); *The Good Society* (New York: Alfred A. Knopf, 1992).

27. David J. Nygren and Miriam D. Ukeritis, *The Future of Religious Orders in the United States* (Westport, Connecticut: Praeger, 1993) 244-247.

28. Cf. Margaret Miles, *Practicing Christianity* (New York: Crossroad, 1988) 152.

Friendship with God

Friendship has a privileged place in the Judeo-Christian tradition.
"God is friendship," writes Aelred of Rievaulx.[29] God reaches out to
us with love and draws us to respond, speaking to us and listening
to us. God shares with us the things that are deepest in the divine
heart and calls us to reciprocate. The stories of God's relationship
with Abraham (Gn 18:17ff) and Moses (Ex 33:11) are paradigmatic
for the Chosen People. Few biblical accounts are more striking than
the beautiful story told in Exodus 33:

> The Lord said to Moses, "Tell the Israelites: You are a
> stiff-necked people. Were I to go up in your company even for
> a moment, I would exterminate you."
> Whenever Moses went out to the tent, the people would all rise
> and stand at the entrance of their own tents, watching Moses
> until he entered the tent. The Lord used to speak to Moses face
> to face, as one person speaks to another.
> Moses said to the Lord, "You, indeed, are telling me to lead this
> people on; but you have not let me know whom you will send
> with me. Yet you have said, 'You are my intimate friend,' and
> also, 'You have found favor with me.' Now, if I have found favor
> with you, do let me know your ways so that, in knowing you, I
> may continue to find favor with you. Then, too, this nation is,
> after all, your own people." "I myself," the Lord answered, "will
> go along, to give you rest." Moses replied, "If you are not going
> yourself, do not make us go up from here. For how can it be
> known that we, your people and I, have found favor with you,
> except by your going with us? Then we, your people and I, will
> be singled out from every other people on the earth." The Lord
> said to Moses, "This request, too, which you have just made, I
> will carry out, because you have found favor with me and you
> are my intimate friend." (Ex 33:5a, 8, 11a, 12-17)

What is striking about this and other Old Testament stories of

---

29. *De spirituali amicitia* 1:69. Margaret Miles calls Aelred's treatment "the most
positive evaluation of friendship to be found in the history of Christianity." Cf.
M. Miles, *Practicing Christianity*, 149.

God's relationship with his friends is the intimacy that God shares with them: "There was no other prophet like Moses. He knew the Lord face to face" (Dt 34:10). It is clear that attentive listening, honesty in speaking, and deep confidence in providence are the signs that characterize God's intimate friends.

In the New Testament Jesus is the revelation of God's friendship with the whole human race (Ti 3:4). The New Testament does not hesitate to tell us that he forged intimate bonds with a number of his followers. "Jesus loved Martha, and her sister and Lazarus very much" (Jn 11:5). Jesus cries at Lazarus' death, and the crowd remarks: "See how much he loved him!" (Jn 11:35-36). John also recalls Jesus' attachment to his "beloved disciple" (Jn 13:23), who is a faithful friend even to the cross (Jn 19:26-27). Likewise, the gospels leave little doubt about Jesus' closeness to Mary Magdalene. Jesus himself, moreover, tells his disciples quite directly that they are no longer servants but his friends (Jn 15:15), with whom he has felt free to share "everything I have heard from my Father."

Those who live in friendship with the Lord are also called to friendship with one another. The book of the Acts attests to the bonds of friendship (Acts 2:44ff; 4:32) in the early Christian community, even while at the same time honestly recounting the difficulties the first disciples experienced (Acts 15:36-39; cf. Gal 2:11-14). The New Testament model for human friendship is Jesus' love of friendship with us. "Love one another as I have loved you. There is no greater love than this: to lay down one's life for one's friends" (Jn 15:12-13). That is surely a very demanding standard.

But while God's friendship with us in Christ is the New Testament model for human friendship, the converse is also true: abiding, loving human relationships can be an enormous help to us in picturing God as a friend.[30]

---

30. John Carmody, *Living with God—in Good Times and Bad* (New York: Crossroad, 1996) 48. Similarly, Vincent de Paul testified during the beatification process of Francis de Sales: "How good you are, God, my God, how good you are, when there is such gentleness in my Lord, Francis de Sales, your creature" (SV XIII, 78-79).

"Soul friends"

Few things are more important on life's journey than a mature, wise "soul friend." As a picturesque Celtic saying puts it, "Anyone without a soul friend is a body without a head." I will not dwell on this theme at length here since many others have written on it very well.[31]

It is especially useful to speak with a soul friend about our prayer, our intense feelings, our relationships, our joys and sorrows, our problems. "Honest talk" about our sexual struggles, even if we find ourselves embarrassed about them, can be a wonderful relief ("I finally got that out!") and a first step toward integration and healing. Of course, it is imperative that one choose "soul friends" carefully. They should be wise, experienced persons of deep faith. An immature guide can be worse than none at all.

Even apart from formal spiritual direction relationships, there are many others who enter our lives who could be described as true soul friends; at times these may be teachers, counsellors, or companions in a community house. The rich Judeo-Christian tradition is filled with examples of such "informal" soul friends.[32] The list is very long, including such intimate friends as David and Jonathan, Naomi and Ruth, Aquinas and Bonaventure, Philip Neri and Charles Borromeo, to name only a few. Friendships like these "double one's joy and divide one's sorrow," as Francis Bacon said.[33]

"Just plain friends"

There are other persons who play an extremely important role in our lives (and to whom, it seems to me, the literature in regard to spirituality sometimes pays little attention). To call them "soul friends" would be too much, since we may never have thought of our relationship with them in terms like that. But they are surely

---

31. Richard McCullen, "Spiritual Direction in the Life of the Priest," *Colloque* (#32; Autumn 1995) 93-114; cf., also, Kenneth Leech, *Soul Friend* (San Francisco: Harper and Row, 1980).
32. Vincent O'Malley, *Saintly Companions* (New York: Alba House, 1995).
33. *The Works of Sir Francis Bacon*, edited by the English Department of the Carnegie Mellon University (1996), *Essays*, "On Friendship." Bacon's essays can be found on Internet.

friends, wonderful ones in fact, people with whom we may at times share thoughts that we reveal to no one else and who are our companions in many of life's joys and sorrows. Without ever analyzing the matter systematically, we easily distinguish such friends from simple comrades whom we like to be with on occasion or whose interests we sometimes share.

Intimate, long-lived, mature friendships are much rarer than simple camaraderie. They sometimes begin by a mere chance happening and ignite quite spontaneously, quickly touching the deepest parts of our person. At other times such genuine friendships develop slowly between spouses, brothers and sisters, parents and children. If, in our mind's eye, we picture lovers standing face to face, our image for faithful friends envisions them walking side by side with us (sometimes, of course, as with spouses who are genuine friends, these two images are applicable to the same persons, but this is not always the case).

We sense within ourselves a deeply appreciative love of such friends even, and perhaps especially, when we know their faults and they know ours. Their number will never be great; in fact, we can count ourselves blessed when they are a small group. C. S. Lewis gives us a striking description of the union of such friends:

> In a perfect Friendship this Appreciative Love is, I think, often so great and so firmly based that each member of the circle feels, in his secret heart, humbled before all the rest. Sometimes he wonders what he is doing there among his betters. He is lucky beyond desert to be in such company. Especially when the whole group is together, each bringing out all that is best, wisest, or funniest in all the others . . . when the whole world, and something beyond the world, opens itself to our minds as we talk; and no one has any claim on or any responsibility for another, but all are freemen and equals as if we had first met an hour ago, while at the same time an Affection mellowed by the years enfolds us. Life—natural life has no better gift to give. Who could have deserved it?[34]

The scriptures sing the praises of faithful friendships. Ben Sirach

---

34. C. S. Lewis, *The Four Loves* (London: Harper Collins, 1977) 67-68.

tells us: "A faithful friend is a sturdy shelter; the person who finds one finds treasure" (Sir 6:14). Great thinkers like Plato, Aristotle and Cicero have sought to analyze such friendships in great detail.

Signs of Genuine Friendship

Friends are surely one of life's greatest gifts. I offer here a few signs of the joyful, healthy, loving relationship that we call friendship.

Deep mutual resonance

Aristotle tells us that a friend is "a second self."[35] "What is friendship?" he asks. "A single soul in two bodies," he responds. Shakespeare expresses the same idea beautifully in *A Midsummer Night's Dream*:

> So we grew together
> Like to a double cherry, seeming parted
> But yet an union in partition,
> Two lovely berries moulded on one stem,
> So with two seeming bodies but one heart.[36]

Similarly, a lovely passage in the Book of Samuel describes the relationship of David and Jonathan: "By the time David finished speaking with Saul, Jonathan had become as fond of David as if his life depended on him; he loved him as he loved himself" (1 Sam 18:1).

Conversely, it is sad to say that there are friendships which are feigned and others which fail, even when there seems to be deep mutual resonance. With great irony Matthew's gospel has Jesus addressing Judas as "friend" (Mt 26:50) at the moment when the apostle betrays him with a kiss in the garden. Surely all of us have painfully witnessed seemingly very close friendships betrayed or suddenly dissolved. In some cases I have known, money (one of the motives the New Testament suggests in regard to Judas) and sexual

---

35. Aristotle, *Nicomachean Ethics*, Book VIII. Aristotle's works can be found on Internet.
36. William Shakespeare, *A Midsummer Night's Dream*, Act III, Scene 1.

infidelity (the taking of a friend's husband or wife) have been among the principal causes of ruptured friendships. I have also known business "friendships" which had lasted for long years, but which quickly dissolved over disputes about the bottom line. In reflective moments, I have asked myself whether such relationships were ever really genuine friendships at all. I have heard many a person refer to another as his "good friend" when I wondered whether they were merely "useful" acquaintances and not really friends in the true sense.

Open communication

Opening one's heart is the key to friendship, noted Francis Bacon.[37] Friends speak freely with one another. They share each other's joys and sorrows, hopes and fears. Sometimes their mutual knowledge is quite intuitive. They know long before the revelation that something painful has happened or that a wonderful event is about to occur. In that sense, friends have common "vibes," as young people put it today, or "mutual resonance," as described above. They know each other so well that they read non-verbal signs long before words disclose what is happening. But eventually, even if there is sometimes delay and patient waiting, friends speak very simply with one another. They say what is in their hearts. Genuine friends can offer critical opinions freely (they are even expected to do so!) because of the confidence that undergirds the relationship. Dorothy Osborne once wrote to William Temple: "You must always tell me freely of anything you see amiss in me, whether I am too stately or not enough, what humor pleases you and what does not, what you would have me do and what avoid, with the same freedom that you would use with a person over whom you had an absolute power . . . ; these are the laws of friendship as I understand them, and I believe I understand them right, for I am certain nobody can be more perfectly a friend than I am yours."[38]

---

37. *The Works of Sir Francis Bacon*, *Essays*, "On Friendship." These essays can be found on Internet.
38. Dorothy Osborne to William Temple, July 2, 1653, in D. J. Enright and David Rawlinson (eds.), *The Oxford Book of Friendship* (New York: Oxford University Press, 1991) 132.

People have often noted that, even after they have revealed embarrassing aspects of themselves to a close friend, mutual esteem has grown between them rather than diminished. In thus speaking simply, a friend is frequently not seeking advice but rather only the understanding of the other, the fitting of some puzzling event into a context, the reflecting back of his own thoughts or perhaps the simple reactions of a concerned other. In that sense, as the English proverb puts it, a good friend is the best mirror.

Positive traits

C. S. Lewis once wrote: "In each of my friends there is something that only some other friend can fully bring out."[39] We have all seen this happen again and again. Surely in the gospel narratives Jesus brings out a hidden beauty in Mary Magdalene. He nourishes a contemplative dimension in Mary, the sister of Martha and Lazarus. I have known very serious people whom a particular friend could easily make laugh. I knew a foul-mouthed man who spoke only the most reverent English in the presence of a woman friend. I have known people who learned to pray only because they were drawn to pray by their friends.

Conversely, of course, immature friendships often reinforce our weakness. How often in contemporary society one witnesses "friends" who become partners in excessive drinking or drugs. How often a person's circle fosters a "consumer" lifestyle or irresponsible sexual behavior.

Resilience

No friendship is without its ups and downs. Even good friends, at times, hurt each other. It is very important, as Samuel Johnson once observed, that someone "keep his friendship *in constant repair*."[40] Because genuine friendships are solid, they do not easily break. Friends bounce back from setbacks and reestablish the mutual

---

39. C. S. Lewis, *The Four Loves*, 58.
40. James Boswell, *Life of Samuel Johnson*, edited by Jack Lynch (Oxford: Clarendon, 1904), year 1755. Boswell's work is now available on Internet.

respect and confidence that might temporarily have been damaged. At the end of a scene in *Middlemarch,* George Eliot places these words in the mouths of the characters:

"I did not mean to quarrel" said Rosamond, putting on her hat.

"Quarrel? Nonsense; we have not quarreled. If one is not to get into a rage sometimes, what is the good of being friends?"[41]

Mature friends know how to disagree, to express anger, to stand firm at times, to give in at other times, to affirm, to criticize, to ask forgiveness humbly.

Endurance

Because of its resilience, friendship endures, not only throughout life but beyond it.

The ongoing Christian tradition assures us that friendship, like all love, is abiding, breaking the bonds of death. The author of Hebrews encourages us with the image of the "great cloud of witnesses" (Heb 12:1) that surrounds us. Christian creeds profess that we believe in the "communion of saints." And Catholic practice from the earliest times has encouraged us to forge trusting friendships with the saints. How many Christians through the centuries, men and women of all social strata, have loved Mary the mother of Jesus and sensed her love for them. How many have had "special saints" with whom they could speak about their daily cares and needs and in whose support they had the greatest confidence. How many have believed deeply in the abiding presence of those who have "gone before us with the sign of faith," parents, brothers and sisters, close friends, who surround us as we celebrate the eucharist and are there encouraging us as we pour out our hearts in silent prayer.[42]

---

41. George Eliot, *Middlemarch: A Study of Provincial Life* (New York: H. M. Caldwell, 1900), I:120-21.
42. Of course, the loss of friends can produce terrible grief. Cf. W. H. Auden's "Funeral Blues" in *Tell Me the Truth About Love, Ten Poems by W. H. Auden* (London: Faber and Faber: 1994) 29:

Freedom

We choose our friends freely. There really is a choice, in spite of what the very romantic sometimes think. The challenge is to choose friends well. Experience teaches that we become like our friends, for better or for worse. Parents are always alarmed when their children keep bad company because they instinctively know that all of us breathe the air that surrounds us and absorb both its beneficial and malignant contents.

It is important not only that we choose friends freely, but also that ample freedom be maintained throughout the relationship. Friends should be able to challenge one another without fearing a rupture of the relationship. They should be able to act freely too, not being so absorbed in one another that their liberty to reach out to others is impeded.

It is here that the "particular friendships" described by Saint Vincent, or what we might today call "protective partnerships," can be especially damaging. Usually these involve a relationship in which two people reinforce an unhealthy dependence on one another and protect each other from outside criticism challenging them to grow. The relationship becomes self-absorbing and isolating. Often the persons involved confirm one another's weaknesses rather than their strengths. Their union with one another becomes a chain rather than a source of liberating energy. Though I must admit that I find seventeenth-century rhetoric about particular friendships excessive at times, nonetheless I am very aware of the reality this rhetoric attempted to express. Twice during the past year I was involved with cases of friends seeking dispensations from their vows on the same day. I ask myself: Did they build up one another's strengths or reinforce each other's weaknesses?

Francis de Sales encourages us, when choosing our friends, to pick "the virtuous."[43]

He was my North, my South, my East, and West,
My working week and my Sunday rest,
My noon, my midnight, my talk, my song;
I thought that love would last for ever: I was wrong.

43. Francis de Sales, *Introduction to a Devout Life*, translated by John K. Ryan (New York: Doubleday Image Book, 1989) Part III, 19, "True Friendship," 174.

In joy and sorrow

A lovely story is told about Oscar Wilde:

> When my father died in 1885 my mother nearly went mad with grief. She shut herself up, refusing to see her friends in a dumb despair.
>
> One afternoon Oscar called: I told him of her desperate state, and he said he must see her. She stubbornly refused, and I went back to him to say I could not prevail on her. "But she must see me," he replied. "She must. Tell her I shall stay here till she does." Back I went, and for a few minutes my mother sat, crying and wringing her hands, and saying "I can't. Send him away." Then she arose and went into the room where he was waiting, crying as she went. I saw Oscar take both her hands and draw her to a chair, beside which he set his own; then I left them alone. He stayed a long time, and before he went I heard my mother laughing.
>
> When he had gone she was a woman transformed. He had made her talk; had asked questions about my father's last illness and allowed her to unburden her heart of those torturing memories. Gradually he had talked of my father, of his music, of the possibilities of a memorial exhibition of his pictures. Then, she didn't know how, he had begun to tell her all sorts of things which he contrived to make interesting and amusing. "And then I laughed," she said. "I thought I should never laugh again.[44]

Little more need be said beyond this touching story. A faithful friend knows how to "rejoice with those who rejoice and weep with those who weep" (Rm 12:15).

A Few Concluding Remarks

Few things are more valuable than friendship. Divine friendship, intimacy, and love are the good news. God's covenant of friendship extends from the greatest to the least, but especially to the poor, to

---

44. H. M. Swanwick (Helena Sickert) *I Have Been Young* (1935), in *Oxford Book of Friendship*, 136-37.

the most abandoned, to those who know how to long for it humbly.

On the human journey a wise "soul friend" is also of incalculable help. I know that my own life would have been very different if it had not been for the at times liberating, at times firm, and always understanding support of the same spiritual director for three decades.

And of course those who are "just plain friends" are a huge blessing in life. Some of my own are companions from the seminary whose friendship has lasted all these years. Others are older; still others, younger. The beginnings of such friendships are hard to define except to say that there was always a common interest of some sort. Sometimes, in my own experience, it was work, sometimes studies (talking about theology!), sometimes sports, sometimes spirituality, sometimes books, sometimes films.

There is lots of laughter and fun in good friendships. I can recall laughing even to tears on occasion. Some of the most enjoyable, relaxing times in my life have been with my friends.

It is clear to me that friendship knows no age limits. One of my closest friends is a former teacher of mine; a seventeen-year age difference separates us. Another was my student; more than twenty years in the other direction separate us. Several others are "of my own time," so to speak.

Nor does gender seem to be a distinguishing factor in friendship, even if it is sometimes a complicating one. Two of the closest friendships that have developed in my own life are with women. They come from completely different continents and from starkly contrasting socio-economic backgrounds. Temperamentally, they differ very greatly, one being unusually serious and private as a person, the other being more joyful and expansive. Their contrast reminds me of Louise de Marillac and Madame Goussault!

What is surely common in all friendships is this: we *like* to be with our friends. They are a source of joy in our lives. The key to this "pleasure," so to speak, is the ability to be free in one another's presence. There is no need, between friends, to pose. You can be yourself. You can say things honestly, as they are. In that sense, there is a great simplicity about friendship. In being oneself, one recognizes, in friends, "a kindred spirit." Even though two friends may have strikingly different characteristics, there is something vital that they hold in common. That is why Shakespeare could describe them as having "two seeming bodies but one heart."

Hilaire Belloc once wrote: "There is nothing worth the wear of winning but the laughter and love of friends."[45] We shall surely laugh with the Lord and our friends in the kingdom (cf. Lk 6:21; Rev 21:4). It is a gift if we can do so now too.

---

45. Hilaire Belloc, *Complete Verse*, with a preface by W. N. Roughhead (London: Gerald Duckworth, 1970) "Dedicatory Ode," 60.

A Time for Building Community

Community Living in the Vincentian Family[1]

Be united with one another, and God will bless you. But let it be by the charity of Jesus Christ, for any union which is not sealed by the blood of our Savior cannot perdure. It is therefore in Jesus Christ, by Jesus Christ, and for Jesus Christ that you ought to be united with one another.[2]

The Present Situation

In recent years, the Vincentian Family has been able to find a considerable number of renewed, creative ways of serving the poor. But it has been more difficult to find ways of significantly renewing community living.

Many of the practices and structures that gave shape to community living in an earlier era have disappeared. Returning to them now would be impossible in most cases. Most of them served their purpose in their own time, but gradually became over-formalized, inflexible, and out-dated. Still, they often aimed at values that have abiding validity: unity with one another, common vision and energy in the apostolate, prayer, penance, and conversion.

With the passing of former practices, we have not yet, unfortunately, come up with sufficient contemporary means for forming communities that are fully alive and attractive to the young.

The Creation of Community—Its Various Levels

We should not be surprised that community is very imperfect at times. If community really is something we must work *toward*, then it can never be captured once for all. We must always be striving to

1. Talk originally given to provincial leaders of the Daughters of Charity in the United States, Fall 1995.
2. Abelly, Book II, chap. 1, 145.

143

create it. Sometimes there will be high points, sometimes lows. We will have better community in one house than in another. We will have better community in some matters than in others. I say this because, as Bernard Lonergan points out, community demands union on many levels, some of which may be better realized than others. Lonergan speaks of four levels at which the bonds of community are forged.[3]

Common experience

Common experience lays the groundwork for community. It is what initial and on-going formation programs try to create. It involves imbibing a common heritage, sharing in common traditions, learning a body of common knowledge through our studies, participating in common symbolic acts, being immersed in and reflecting together on common works, living a common lifestyle.

When people first come together, they often do not have much common experience. So it must be worked at. A person who has spent most of a lifetime in hospitals may find little in common with someone who has spent much of the time teaching small children. When they enter a local community together, they will have to work hard at making community real.

Common understanding

Common understanding means that when we *say* the same things we *mean* the same things. Take sin, for example. For one person it may mean breaking a law. For another it may mean breaking a relationship. For one person God may be a judge. For another God may be a loving father or mother. For still a third, God may be the sum total of world forces. One person may view the Church as a predominantly hierarchical institution where new directions come mainly from above. Another may see the Church as the people of God where new ideas bubble up from below. For these people to come to a common understanding (and they will never perfectly achieve that goal) will demand much dialogue.

---

3. Bernard Lonergan, *A Third Collection* (Mahwah, N.J.: Paulist Press, 1985) 5-6.

Common judgment

This means that we come to agree, as a community, on certain ideas. "We hold these truths"; e.g., those contained in a constitution. For example, the Daughters of Charity as a body hold that the end of the Company is to honor Christ as the source of all charity, serving him corporally and spiritually in the person of the poor. When a new member comes to join the community, he or she must assimilate the basic common judgments that are *foundational* to the community. There will also be many other more concrete, practical common judgments that particular local communities come to agree on; e.g., that they will assist at the eucharist together each day in the parish church; that the best time for this is at seven o'clock in the morning; that their lifestyle should be simple, and at the same time warm and family-like; that they will work both in a school and in a parish; etc. Reaching common judgments demands meetings, a decision-making process, a willingness to compromise, and respect for differing opinions. Even in the best of times, however, disagreements over judgments, and especially over means, will remain. The body of *foundational* common judgments will not be excessively detailed, nor very large; moreover, while the most basic truths will remain stable, their interpretation will never be static.

Common action

A community must act together on the judgments which it has made. The members must work with one another in such a way that they feel co-responsibility. If the community merely has common experiences, common understanding, and common judgments, but its members do not carry them into action, then it is not a true community. It lacks follow-through. It is in agreement ideologically, but not committed in actuality.

The commitment to obedience, which has played a part in all Christian communities, comes into play on this level. Members of a community must be resolved that after consultation and dialogue, they will work together in acting on common judgments, even if some (or even many) continue to hold dissenting views (cf. C 2.8).

Obedient, loving dissent is a healthy reality in community and can provide the basis for on-going dialogue. As Socrates pointed out, dissent is a function of loyalty to the group, even if at times it may create some discomfort for the members. But even those who hold dissenting views should be willing to cooperate in obedience.

In summary, true community involves all four levels: common experience, common understanding, common judgment and common action. Sometimes these will be more fully realized; at other times, less fully.

Five Community Moments

But it is always important to speak about community concretely. Dietrich Bonhoeffer once said: "The person who loves her dream of community more than the real community itself destroys community."[4]

Community exists when we live it vitally. Let me dwell briefly on five significant moments in community living. They are the building-blocks, so to speak, of local communities.

Meals

It might seem strange that I begin with eating. My focus, however, is not on food (though Saint Vincent did encourage treasurers to serve good wine and good bread [SV III, 505]). My focus is on common meals as one of the primary signs of union. When asked what are the most striking memories of their families, countless people respond by describing long festive dinners at Christmas or Easter in which people sat around the table telling stories, or a time together on vacation where everyone ate together, relaxed, sang, played games, and talked until late into the night. Of course, not every meal can be that way. But meals are a prime time for good human communication. They are times when our tradition is deepened because we recall stories from the past and speak of wonderful men and women whom we have known. They are a time when that

4. D. Bonhoeffer, *Life Together* (London: SCM Press, 1954) 15.

tradition is developed because new people express new insights and new ways of responding to the same values in the service of the poor.

Crucial in the human conversation that characterizes meals is attentive listening. We must be deeply interested in one another, in our backgrounds, our histories, our gifts, the projects that set us on fire. Few things are worse than having an exciting experience to relate, bringing it up at table, and finding that no one seems eager to hear it.

Essential too is simple dialogue, the ability to elicit further feelings and thoughts, to pose helpful questions, to give one's own reaction without being either defensive or aggressive.

In the past, meals were usually fully occupied with reading at table. Today they are an opportunity for genuine, interested conversation.

Of course, the eucharistic meal plays a most significant role here too. It is a time for attentive listening to the word of God, for genuine sharing in faith, and for union in the life of the Lord. Some of my striking memories in community have been wonderful eucharistic celebrations.

Prayer

Here let me mention three distinctive moments.

a) Our common liturgical prayer. It is very important that it be prepared well and celebrated beautifully and meditatively. If so, it can be a most significant means of our contact with God and with one another, a time when we cry out:

> It is good to give thanks to the Lord,
> to make music to your name, O most High,
> to proclaim your love in the morning
> and your truth in the watches of the night. (Ps 92:2-3)

b) Faith sharing. This is one of the most common contemporary forms that the traditional "repetition of prayer" is taking (C 2.14). It can be a powerful moment in building community if the members are capable of sharing their faith with great simplicity. Faith sharing is not meant to be a homily prepared ahead of time, nor is it meant to be a catharsis for releasing one's pent-up anxieties, but rather it is a spontaneous expression of what happens as one lives and prays. We can strengthen each other by sharing our faith.

c) Mental prayer. Mental prayer can seem a rather solitary exercise, but we engage in it *together* in order to support one another in reflecting on God's word and in contemplating his presence. Personally, I sense that support very much; I am encouraged when I find myself meditating with my brothers and sisters. Conversely, I am quite discouraged when I find myself alone in the chapel, wondering where everybody else is. If the liturgy is "the summit toward which the activity of the Church is directed,"[5] mental prayer is one of the key foundation stones. It nourishes and strengthens our faith. It is important, therefore, that we support one another in engaging in it.

Fun

If prayer is the human heart searching for God, humor helps us to realize that God is unpredictable, as are most of us, his creatures!

It is very important to have fun in community. Fun fosters harmony by preventing us from being overly serious about ourselves. Just as it is important that the community work together, so also it is important that it relax together and laugh from time to time. In that way we enjoy one another. We see different aspects of each other's personality.

Humor is linked to our perception of incongruity. There is lots that is incongruous in our lives, if only we can see it with a little bit of distance.

A local community should be creative in organizing times of diversion. I lived in a house where once a week, at night, we watched a videotape of a movie together. We agreed on the film ahead of time. Somebody prepared a few snacks, and we sat around and talked about it afterwards. I loved it, and so did everybody else. Nobody had to come, but everybody did.

---

5. *The Constitution on the Sacred Liturgy* 10.

There are many other possibilities, but it is very important that we enjoy each other's company, laugh, relax, and at times simply have fun.

Meetings

Even though meetings are sometimes a scourge in our lives, or as I have suggested elsewhere, one of the contemporary forms of mortification, nonetheless, they are a very important community moment. They are a time when much important communication takes place. They should be a moment in which everyone feels included, in which people feel a common responsibility for the values being shared and the decisions being made.

I suggest that two meetings are of particular importance:

a) The meeting for formulating the local community plan (C 3.46; S 57). Unfortunately, many houses still do this very poorly. They tend to make it more like an occasion for deciding on an order of day, rather than a time for creativity. They are slow to exercise the flexibility that the Constitutions and Statutes provide. But the meeting for formulating the local community plan can be precisely the time in which these "moments of community" that I am describing can be developed, enriched, and covenanted. I encourage you as provincial leaders to assist local communities in developing their plans.

b. Meetings for evaluation or *revision de vie* (C 2.14; S 1, 4, 5). We seek ongoing communal conversion within community. Evaluation times give us an opportunity to reflect on our lifestyle and on our mission. It is important that we do this honestly and peacefully. Such meetings can be the time for many suggestions that can be helpful for the growth of a local community. At the same time, I encourage you to avoid "guilt trips." I have been at endless meetings, in rather exemplary communities, in which people agonized over eating too well, or spending too much money, when, in fact, the community lived with rather great simplicity. I alluded earlier to the lovely letter in which Saint Vincent encourages the local treasurer to provide good bread and good wine for the members of the house.

"Without that," he says, "they will be grumbling much of the time and will not work effectively apostolically." The key point here is balance. One must seek to balance simplicity of life with simple joys.

Apostolate

The Vincentians and the Daughters of Charity are apostolic *societies*. Our apostolate, therefore, has a communal dimension. I encourage you, therefore, to plan in common, to evaluate in common, and actually to work with one another as a team in your apostolates as much as possible. There are few things that tie us together more than cooperating in an exciting common project. It is wonderful when, in a healthy sense, we are proud of what we do in a hospital or in a school or in a parish center. A good common work is a strong unifying force.

Dietrich Bonhoeffer, who experienced a martyr's death in a German prison camp at the very end of World War II, wrote this about community:

> Between the death of Christ and the Last Day it is only by a gracious anticipation of the last things that Christians are privileged to live in visible fellowship with other Christians. It is by the grace of God that a congregation is permitted to gather visibly in this world to share God's word and sacrament. Not all Christians receive this blessing. The imprisoned, the sick, the scattered lonely, the proclaimers of the gospel in heathen lands stand alone. They know that visible fellowship is a blessing. They remember, as the Psalmist did, how they went "with the multitude . . . to the house of God, singing with joy and praise" (Ps 42:4).[6]

---

6. Bonhoeffer, *Life Together*, 8.

A Time for Meditating

On Some Aspects of the Humanity of Jesus[1]

Do you remember the wonderful incident in John's fourteenth chapter? Philip comes to Jesus and says, "Lord, show us the Father, and that will be enough for us" (Jn 14:8). Jesus answers, "Philip, have I been with you for so long a time and you still do not know me? Whoever has seen me has seen the Father."

The way we know God our Father is by contemplating the humanity of Jesus. The author of the *Imitation of Christ* puts it this way: "Let all the study of our heart be from now on to have our meditation fixed wholly on the life of Christ." So, if we want to know what God is like we must focus on the humanity of Jesus. He is the word made flesh, the revelation of God himself.

Saint Vincent knew this lesson very well. He tells us that Jesus is our only rule. He urges the Vincentians: "Let us walk with confidence on this royal road on which Jesus Christ will be our mentor and guide" (SV XI, 53).

As we begin this new year today, may I ask you to join with me in meditating on the humanity of Jesus. Mary his mother, whose feast we celebrate today, was fascinated by her newborn child and pondered the events of his birth. Luke's gospel, in fact, tells us that she "kept all these things in her heart, reflecting on them" (cf. Lk 2:19; 2:51). I encourage you to make these first days of the year a time when, with Mary, you contemplate Jesus in the flesh.

I choose today only certain aspects of the humanity of Jesus, those which strike me most forcefully.

Jesus' Deep Human Love

In John's gospel and letters, this is what God is all about. "God is love" (1 Jn 3:16). He reveals this love in Jesus. What is this love like? It is, as Saint Vincent would put it, both affective and effective.

---

1. Talk originally given to the Daughters of Charity at the Motherhouse in Paris, January 1, 1996.

Affective

Notice the details in the Lazarus story in John's eleventh chapter.

> Now a man was ill, Lazarus from Bethany, the village of Mary and her sister Martha. Jesus loved Martha and her sister and Lazarus. When he arrived, he found that Lazarus had already been in the tomb for four days. When Mary came to where Jesus was and saw him she fell at this feet and said to him, "Lord, if you had been here, my brother would not have died." When Jesus saw her weeping and the Jews who had come with her weeping, he became perturbed and deeply troubled, and said, "Where have you laid him?" They said to him, "Sir, come and see." And Jesus wept. So the Jews said, "See how he loved him." (Jn 11:1, 5, 17, 32-36)

Jesus cared deeply. He loved with a sensitive, human love that touched his friends. Martha and Mary and Lazarus knew that he loved them, as did John, who even described himself as the disciple whom Jesus loved. With this same love Jesus reaches out to the widow of Naim (Lk 7:11) and has compassion on her at the death of her son. With this same love he feels for a married couple at Cana when they have no wine (Jn 2:1-11). With this same love he has pity on the crowds because they are wandering and aimless like sheep without a shepherd (Mt 9:35-38). It is an affective, caring, compassionate love.

Effective

But in the New Testament, Jesus' love is also quite effective. It is love in deed and in truth (1 Jn 3:18). Let me concretize three ways especially in which Jesus' love shows itself as effective:

Service

Mutual service is fundamental in the community of Jesus' followers. Jesus proclaims the importance of service by his person (he is the suffering servant) and by his words.

This theme was closest to Jesus' heart as he began the farewell discourse in John's gospel: "Before the feast of Passover, Jesus knew that his hour had come to pass from this world to the Father. He loved his own in the world and he loved them to the end" (Jn 13:1-20). Jesus then washes his followers' feet. Then he says: "I have given you a model to follow, so that as I have done for you, you should also do." Love within the community of Jesus' disciples is to be an everyday, practical love that is eager not so much to be served as to serve.

Sacrifice

"In this is love," John writes, "that he laid down his life for us; so we are to lay down our lives for our brothers and sisters" (1 Jn 3:16). "Love, then, consists in this: not that we have loved God, but that he first loved us and has sent his Son as an offering for our sins" (1 Jn 4:10). When Paul writes to Timothy, he says: "Look to Jesus, the self-giving one" (1 Tim 2:6; cf. Gal 2:20; Eph 5:1-2). It is in giving over his life that Jesus showed his love most effectively to his followers.

Friendship

The gospels make explicit what I have already implied; namely, that Jesus forged strong bonds of friendship. I encourage you today to meditate on the words of John's fifteenth chapter: "There is no greater love than this: to lay down one's life for one's friends. You are my friends if you do what I command you. I no longer speak of you as slaves, for a slave does not know what his master is about. Instead, I call you friends, since I have made known to you all that I have heard from my Father" (Jn 15:13-15).

The apostles experienced that Jesus had befriended them. This was so too with Martha and Mary and Lazarus. He takes us also, John assures us, as his friends, to whom he opens his heart. He shares with us his words, his love, his life.

Jesus' Anxiety about the Future and His Determination to do the Father's Will

John's gospel often smooths over Jesus' anxieties, but in his twelfth chapter John makes no attempt to hide them. "I am troubled now, yet what should I say? 'Father, save me from this hour?' But it was for this purpose that I came to this hour. Father, glorify your name" (Jn 12:27-28). As he came to Jerusalem for the last time, the future loomed large before Jesus, with ever more threatening shadows. All of the gospels describe his pain and anxiety as he began to face the prospect of betrayal and death. Mark's gospel speaks graphically: "He took with him Peter, James, and John and began to be troubled and distressed. Then he said to them, 'My soul is sorrowful even to death. Remain here and keep watch'" (Mk 14:33-34). He then prays a prayer of deep human anxiety: "Abba, Father, all things are possible to you. Take this cup away from me, but not what I will but what you will" (Mk 14:36). In case we are tempted to think of Jesus as always cool and serene, Luke reminds us that, in the garden, his sweat became like drops of blood falling on the ground (Lk 22:44). The author of Hebrews reminds us how human Jesus was at this moment: "In the days when he was in the flesh, he offered prayers and supplications with loud cries and tears to the one who is able to save him from death, and he was heard because of his reverence. Son though he was, he learned obedience from what he suffered" (Heb 5:7-8).

Notice how human Jesus' experience is. He struggles to accept the Father's will. In this, he is very much "one" with us.

Jesus' Prayer

Prayer is a wonderfully human act. It is an expression of our dependence on God. It is also highly personal, relational. It is the kind of deep communication that takes place between friends.

John's gospel loves to tell us about Jesus' conversations with his Father. Luke's gospel, in order to instruct us how to be disciples, takes pains to describe how Jesus prayed. Let me paint the Lukan picture for you very schematically:

- he prays at his baptism (3:21)
- he withdraws to pray alone (5:16)
- he prays before he chooses the twelve (6:12)
- he prays before Peter's confession (9:18)
- he prays before the transfiguration (9:29)

- he tells his followers to pray for laborers for the harvest (10:2)
- he praises the Father for revealing himself to the humble (10:21)
- he teaches the disciples to pray (11:1)
- he tells two parables on prayer (11:5)
- he teaches them perseverance in prayer (18:1)
- he teaches them humility in prayer (18:9)
- he prays at the Last Supper, to strengthen Peter's faith (22:32)
- he prays during his agony in the garden (22:41-42)
- "Father, forgive them, they know not what they do" (23:34)
- "Father, into your hands I commend my spirit" (23:46)

Jesus stands before God in continual dialogue, because that is what human existence is all about. He calls us his followers to enter into the same kind of loving relationship with the giver of all life.

There are few things more important than meditating on the humanity of Jesus. "I am the way, the truth, and the life," Jesus tells us, "no one comes to the Father but through me" (Jn 14:6). Knowing Jesus is to know that Father. I do not offer you here concrete steps for loving Jesus or serving the poor. I simply ask you to focus on Jesus and let him capture your heart more and more. He will teach you everything.

My prayer for each of you is that you will have no other rule than Jesus himself and no deeper desire than to be united with him in a bond of intimate love. In taking on human flesh, Jesus wants to enter into friendship with you and me. I encourage you therefore, if I might paraphrase the words of the most famous English poet, "Grapple him to thy soul with hoops of steel."[2]

---

2. Shakespeare, *Hamlet*, Act I, Scene 3.

A Time for Witnessing

A Call to Prophetic Witness
A Reflection on the Document *Vita Consecrata*[1]

Have you met any prophets lately? I met one recently. Let me tell you my story.

I rose at four o'clock in the morning and walked through the dark streets of a Chinese city. I stayed about fifty yards behind my guide, since we did not want to be seen together. After about a mile, I saw a door open suddenly. The guide entered quickly. When I arrived at the same door, it opened and I entered too. Inside, the curtains were drawn so that no one would see us, and we spoke in whispers so that no one would hear. There, we met an elderly woman, about eighty-five years of age. She was delighted to see me, the Superior General of her Vincentian Family. She had remained behind in China when all the foreign Sisters were expelled forty-six years ago. In that period she had surely felt abandoned many times, but she had remained faithful, filled with trust in the Lord while spending twenty years in prison and in a forced labor camp. Five young women arrived in the same apartment a few minutes after me. They want to be Daughters of Charity like her. They come secretly to receive formation from her.

I ask myself: What did this Sister, who is nearly blind and deaf, *do* to attract them? The answer I come up with is this: Really, she *did* almost nothing, but she *lived* with enormous fidelity, joy, and peace, filled with faith in the presence of the Lord. She was, and continues to be, a prophetic witness to the gospels.

---

1. Talk originally given at the Union of Superiors General Assembly, Ariccia, Italy, May 22-25, 1996.

The Vowed Life as Prophecy

The leitmotif of *Vita Consecrata* is that the vows are prophetic witness.

Prophets speak for God. They interpret history. They bring God's word to bear on present-day reality and often judge that reality lacking in light of the kingdom of God. Jesus is the culmination of the prophets. In him the reign of God dawns. He proclaims incessantly: The kingdom of God is at hand. He calls his followers to announce the same good news.

The vowed life too is prophecy. It says to the world that the kingdom of God is here. It is in the service of the kingdom that we vow chastity, poverty, and obedience. It is only because of our faith and hope in the kingdom that we believe that our vows are worthwhile.

To speak more concretely, the vows proclaim that the kingdom of God sets us free. Believe in the power of the kingdom, the vows say.

- Be free to go wherever in the world the needs of the poor call you, rather than to hold on tightly to the security of your own home or a job you like.

- Be free to share your own material possessions with the poor, rather than to store them up for your own comfort.

- Be free to stand with the poor in their struggle for justice, rather than to stand with the "powers that be," who often insulate themselves from the problems of the poor.

- Be free to speak the truth in the face of the social problems of our times, rather than to be concerned about your own image or tranquility.

- Be free to live together in community as friends who love one another, rather than to isolate those who are different because of nationality, race, class, sex, or other factors that create prejudices.

- Be free to spend time in prayer, rather than to feel that you must always be "doing something."

- Be free to discern the will of God with others, to listen well, rather than to dominate or claim a personal monopoly on knowing God's will.

- Be free to renounce immediate gratification for the sake of more important goals, rather than to seek solely what pleases you in the here and now.

- Be free to witness to forms of love that are more lasting than sexual union, rather than to focus on sexual relations as if they were the only way of loving.

If we live the vowed life genuinely, it is a prophetic word in the world. It challenges tendencies that continually reassert themselves in human history (cf. 1 Jn 2:16):

- the imperative that I *must* have more.

- the drive toward uncommitted or abusive sexual relations.

- the hunger to do whatever I want, even when my own will works harm in the lives of others.

A striking thing about the vowed life as prophecy is that it need not even use words. Almost nothing has to be said. The prophecy is proclaimed by our lives. The message is strikingly clear, even if mysterious: the reign of God is at hand. The vowed life says to others: Surely these women and men who live chastity, poverty, obedience, and give their lives in the service of the poor believe in the kingdom of God deeply!

The Truth of the Prophecy

The power of prophecies lies in the truth they teach. They catch the listener's attention because they jar him or her. The truth they proclaim on the one hand does not seem immediately evident ("The kingdom of God is at hand!"), but on the other hand it cries out to be believed ("Look at the signs! Look at the deep faith, hope, and love of those who vow their whole lives to God in the service of the kingdom").

Our vows will be a credible prophecy only if we live them truthfully. Fidelity is the key to the prophecy. The vows are prophetic signs if lived out genuinely to the end. Otherwise they become a scandal, a lie, the story of one who gave but then took back.

A New Context

The mission of every group must be "actualized" in every place and every era; otherwise, the group remains static, and eventually it withers and dies.[2]

Changing circumstances in society make it necessary for communities to adjust their life and mission continually. Recent popes, particularly Paul VI in *Evangelii Nuntiandi* and John Paul II in *Redemptoris Missio,* and now in *Vita Consecrata,* have reminded us of the new challenges that face those engaged in an evangelizing mission. They speak of:

- the "new areopagi";[3] that is, new sectors in which the gospel must be proclaimed such as the world of communication, science, and international relations particularly as the Church seeks to promote peace, human development, and the liberation of peoples.[4]

- new forms of poverty, different from those of other eras, which challenge missionaries as they attempt to give flesh to the Church's preferential option for the poor.[5]

- a new evangelization: new in its ardor, its methods, and its expression.[6]

- new means of communication which are available to

---

2. A number of business corporations are learning this lesson the hard way. Even some which were once thriving concerns are now experiencing death pangs because they did not adjust to rapidly changing economic circumstances.

3. *Vita Consecrata* 96f; *Tertio Millennio Adveniente* 57.

4. *Redemptoris Missio* 37.

5. *Vita Consecrata* 73, 82, 89; *Tertio Millennio Adveniente* 51; *Sollicitudo Rei Socialis* 42.

6. John Paul II, Discourse at the Nineteenth Ordinary Assembly of CELAM, Haiti, March 9, 1983: discourse given in Santo Domingo, October 12, 1984; cf. *Evangelii Nuntiandi* 63; *Centesimus Annus* 5; *Tertio Millennio Adveniente* 45; *Vita Consecrata* 81.

the evangelizer in catechizing, preaching, and teaching, but which also form part of a new "information culture" which is itself badly in need of evangelization.[7]

Living the Vows in North America

In light of these new challenges, which are emphasized repeatedly in a whole series of Church documents, allow me to suggest five priorities for Institutes of Consecrated Life and Societies of Apostolic Life in North America.

1. *A clear preferential option for the poorest of the poor.* These are in large proportion women and small children. They are more likely to be black, native American, or Hispanic. The future of religious life depends on its ministering to the deepest human needs, not only those of the USA but also global needs.[8]

2. *Contact with youth. Organizing groups, especially the young, to join in your experience of God and your service of the poor.* Ministry to young people is extremely important today. The young are the Church of the future. Yet, like the rest of us, they too breathe the air of individualism that pervades North American society. But several recent studies point out that young people in North America seek an experience of God, intense community and solidarity with others, and explicit and worldwide service to the most needy.[9]

I want to encourage North American religious to gather young people together to pray, to support one another in living the gospels, and to share in the Church's preferential option for the poor. Youth groups can take many forms, depending on the local culture and its possibilities, but I urge all to make this one of the priorities in mission.

---

7. *Vita Consecrata* 99; *Evangelii Nuntiandi* 45; *Redemptoris Missio* 47.
8. D. Nygren and M. Ukeritis, *The Future of Religious Orders in the United States* (Connecticut: Praeger Press, 1993) 235, 244, 251.
9. Cf. Albert di Ianni, "Religious Vocations: New Signs of the Times," *Review for Religious* 52 (#5; September-October 1993) 745-63. Also, Nygren and Ukeritis, *Future of Religious Orders*, 251.

3. *Solidarity with women in their struggle for justice.* Women are discriminated against in almost all parts of the world. In North America the struggle for their rights is strong, articulate, and sometimes even bitter. As in all struggles, there can be extreme reactions on all sides. The real issues are at times confused with false ones. Sometimes we lack the proper categories, the correct distinctions, even the right vocabulary to deal with the problem (as is the case with English possessive pronouns!). The document urges us to take "concrete steps, beginning by *providing room for women to participate* in different fields and at all levels, including decision-making processes, above all in matters which concern women themselves."[10] Implementing this recommendation concretely will be no small task.

4. *Promotion of vocations to Institutes of Consecrated Life and Societies of Apostolic Life.* The lack of vocations to communities in the United States and Canada is critical. And like any critical malady it can develop into a life and death issue for the Church in those countries.

One of the signs of our love for and our happiness in our vocation is the encouragement of others to join in our common life and mission.

The world has seen dramatic changes in the last forty years. Formerly a Catholic culture and closely-knit stable Catholic families strongly supported vocations to the vowed life. Today, on the contrary, many of the structures that were formerly supportive of vocations have disappeared. Families are very small and are often broken. A "Catholic" culture has given way to an "information" culture in which the media often flood young people with a proclamation of values that have little to do with the gospel. We cannot remain passive in such a context. Vocations will not just come along by themselves.

5. *Penetrating the world of the media.* Have you seen "Dead Man Walking"? The film is, by and large, the conversation between a prisoner and a sister. Both Susan Sarandon, who won the Academy Award, and Sean Penn, who was nominated for one, speak in glowing terms of their contact with Sr. Helen Prejean, C.S.J., who

---

10. *Vita Consecrata* 58.

was the actual Sister who visited the prisoner on death row in Louisiana. Both the actress and the actor confess that she had a powerful impact on their lives. The media can be a powerful force for good, but unfortunately they sometimes promote values that are hostile to the gospels: unrestrained violence, irresponsible or "dream-like" sex, the need always to have more and to have it immediately, the right to do what I want to do, even if my own desires conflict with the rights, or at times the lives, of others.

Vita Consecrata suggests, as have many other recent Church documents, that we must learn the language of the media, that we must know how to influence it and change it, that we must be capable of channeling the power of the media toward genuine human values. The United States is, in a sense, the media capital of the world. Nowhere is this challenge more imperative than there.

The Signs of the Prophet

How will we recognize the prophets? What are the signs that they are fully alive among us? Let me list five briefly.

1. *The prophets radiate transcendence.* If the prophet is one who speaks for God, then surely the clearest sign of prophetic authenticity is that we see God in him or her.

2. *They have vital contact with dire human need.* "The blind see, the lame walk, the poor have the good news preached to them." Prophets not only cry out for justice, they walk alongside the poor in the journey toward liberation.

3. *They live in solidarity with others.* In a world where there is so much individualism, the prophet proclaims co-responsibility, family, integration, the unity of humankind.

4. *They witness to simplicity of life.* Prophets know what is important in life. Their values are clear. They seek the "one thing necessary." Everything else is secondary. For that reason there is a beautiful simplicity in their lives.

5. *They communicate joy.* The joy, the peace of the Lord shines out through the prophets. They sing a new song. The Risen Lord rings in their words and in their actions. They are resurrection people with alleluia as their song.

My brothers and sisters, the center of consecrated life is prophetic witness to the kingdom. "Jesus is alive," the prophet says, "he is here." The prophet's life challenges the world to see the Risen Lord.

A Time for Growing in Holiness

Four Themes in the Spirituality of Saint John Gabriel Perboyre

Canonizations are for us. Those heroic men and women whose holiness is "certified" already stand in the presence of God. The Church canonizes them in order to strengthen and encourage the rest of us who continue on our journey.

We have all known uncanonized saints. Our own Vincentian Family has seen thousands and thousands of them, I am sure. Is there anyone among us who has not known a heroic priest who labored tirelessly and sensitively in the service of the most abandoned, or a Daughter of Charity who brought the presence of God to the homes of the sick or who walked the corridors of a hospital bringing the Lord's peace to the dying? Among the uncanonized saints I list a Vincentian brother who shortly before he died talked with me about what the kingdom of God would be like and who throughout his life witnessed to its joy. I also think of a Vincentian layman, a wise lawyer, self-sacrificing, deeply in touch with God. In fact, I am happy to say that, among my brothers and sisters in our family, I have known a number of saints, some of whom are still alive.

But from time to time the Church canonizes saints, holding them up before us as models. It says to us: Look carefully at this man, meditate on this woman, learn from them what it means to be holy.

So it is with John Gabriel Perboyre. On June 2, 1996, he was declared a saint. What does he teach us about living God's life?

Perhaps the most important things have already been said in this regard. In recent months several books and numerous articles have appeared describing Perboyre's years of faithful labor in the formation of priests, his yearning to serve as a missionary in China, his brief, difficult labors there, his sufferings during a year of imprisonment, and his painful death.

---

1. Apostolic Constitution, *Divinus Perfectionis Magister*, introduction.

Here, I will try not to repeat what others have written. The purpose of this chapter is modest. It asks: What went on inside this genuinely holy man? How did he see God? How did he look at his mission? What was his attitude toward those around him? What shape did his prayer-life take? The chapter probes his letters[2] in an attempt to formulate a response, just as many have probed the events of his life and death in order to understand him more fully.[3]

Four themes, especially, stand out in his letters.

Devotion to Providence

"I love the mystery of Providence very much."

Perboyre writes those words to Pierre Le Go (*Letters*, p. 119). His letters make the depth of this love very clear. The mystery of providence, in fact, is a leitmotif that runs through them, a melody that plays in the background, as Perboyre reflects on life's events. His accent on providence is particularly evident in three different settings.

First, God's providence takes the form of a journey-theme in many of Perboyre's letters: God walks with him, protecting him. He asks the Superior General, Dominique Salhorgne, to join with him and his companions in praising "the providence of the heavenly Father" for all the wonderful things that had happened during their trip from Le Havre to Jakarta (*Letters*, p. 101). He writes similarly to others from Surabaya (*Letters*, p. 107) and from Macau (*Letters*, p. 116). But Perboyre is quite concrete about providence. While attributing everything to God, he clearly recognizes that God works through secondary causes (*Letters*, p. 116). He acknowledges therefore that the missionaries owed their safety not only to providence, but to the captain too! During his journeys on foot within China, he was utterly convinced that God was leading him step by step, but he was also grateful to his guides (*Letters*, p. 172). Likewise, while he believed

---

2. Let me thank Fr. Emeric Amyot d'Inville, Sr. Ann Mary Dougherty, Sr. Alicia Muñoz, and Mrs. Anna Carletti, who helped me analyze the themes in Perboyre's letters. Without their assistance this chapter would not have been written.

3. A total of 102 letters were annotated and published by Joseph Van Den Brandt in a very limited edition at Beijing in 1940.

deeply that it was providence which had prepared the way for his whole missionary adventure in China, he also was grateful to his superiors for sending him (*Letters*, p. 211).

Secondly, besides this journey-theme, providence has a further resonance in Perboyre's writings. He sees it as an "order," God's hidden plan. In this sense, like Vincent de Paul, he does not want to "run ahead of it" (*Letters*, p. 23). He tells his brother Louis, just before the latter's departure for China, that God knows how to achieve his goals and how to obtain his greater glory and the sanctification of the elect (*Letters*, p. 41). Perboyre's letter is all the more poignant in that it was their last contact. Louis died on the way, never reaching the goal that he longed for in China. On hearing of his brother's death, John Gabriel writes to his parents: "The providence of God is very gentle, very admirable in regard to his servants, and infinitely more merciful than we can imagine" (*Letters*, p. 53). Years later he writes similarly from China to his cousin, describing the death of a young man to whom he was ministering. He meditates aloud on "the loving care of providence toward her elect, especially when it is a question of the passage to eternity" (*Letters*, p. 258).

Thirdly, it is evident from Perboyre's letters that he sees suffering as a part of the mystery of God's provident love. He is convinced that "God chastises those whom he loves" (*Letters*, p. 61). He states that the life of the missionary is fifty percent suffering (*Letters*, p. 98). He writes to the Superior General from China: "I do not know what is in store for me in the career that is opening up before me: without doubt, many crosses—that is the daily bread of the missionary. But what better can one hope for, when going to preach a crucified God?" (*Letters*, p. 141). This theme deepens as he begins to catch glimpses of the possibility of his own death.

The prospect of martyrdom is not uncommon in his letters. He views it serenely. He tells his father: "If we have to suffer martyrdom, it would be a great grace" (*Letters*, p. 214). He writes to his cousin, "Our Lord always takes care of those who abandon everything for him. It is when they are the most abandoned of men, above all at the moment of death, that he gives them more than the promised hundredfold" (*Letters*, p. 259). He yearns that his own heart might be united with the suffering hearts of Jesus and Mary (*Letters*, p. 260). Not long before his capture, writing to Jean Grappin, Assistant General in Paris, he muses about his own bad health and his future, concluding, "For the rest, I have no great concern about these matters. It is all up to providence!" (*Letters*, p. 284).

Throughout his letters, especially as he speaks of providence, Perboyre's view of God is clear. He sees God as good, gentle, loving. The treasures of God's providence are "inexhaustible" (*Letters*, p. 211). He regards sufferings as "gifts from heaven" (*Letters*, p. 61). In fact, he received many such gifts. His letters attest that he suffered almost continually from bad health in China. Upon his arrival there he was sick for three months and almost died. He often experienced great pain in walking (*Letters*, p. 185). The difficulties caused by his hernia are a frequent theme.

His final letter to his confreres attests to the sufferings he endured during his imprisonment. He was forced to kneel on chains while hanging by his thumbs and hair braid. Besides other tortures which he does not describe, he was struck 110 times. He says discreetly that his readers will find out many other details later, as they surely did when they heard the account of his painful death by strangulation.

His Love for the Mission

"How happy I am for such a wonderful vocation."

This is his exclamation as he announces to his uncle that he is being sent to China (*Letters*, p. 95). Perboyre's enthusiasm for the missions is evident quite early. It is clear that two missionaries who had gone before him were a source of deep inspiration for him: Francis Regis Clet and his own brother Louis.

He frequently mentions Clet. He says to Pierre Le Go: "Might I resemble to the end that venerable confrere whose long apostolic life was crowned with the glorious palm of martyrdom" (*Letters*, p. 119). His letters from China speak of Clet with much admiration. He hopes that his cause of beatification will be promoted. He is eager to visit his burial place. He talks about Clet's long years of ministry, his difficulties in speaking Chinese, his sufferings, his death by strangulation on a cross.

There is a lovely letter written from Surabaya to his uncle in which he speaks about his brother:

> I was not able to make this voyage to China without often thinking about my dear Louis. I loved to consider him walking before me, showing me the road that I should follow. Sad to say, like the star that guided the Magi, he disappeared in the midst of the journey. O what great joy I will experience when I see him once again shining with new brightness and showing me where Jesus, the divine King, lies! (*Letters*, p. 110)

It is clear as early as February 1832 that John Gabriel was eager to take Louis' place as a missionary in China (*Letters*, pp. 54-55). His brother is often mentioned in his correspondence.

After his arrival on the mainland, Perboyre writes rather striking accounts of his new missionary activities. It is evident that he loved the Chinese people (*Letters*, pp. 138, 150). Today, moreover, when we emphasize inculturation so much, it is interesting to note the various ways in which he tried to adapt to Chinese life. First of all, he took on the grooming and the dress of the Chinese. "If you could only see me now," he writes almost laughingly to his brother Jacques, describing what a spectacle he is with his Chinese outfit, his shaved head, his long pigtail and mustache, and his eating with chopsticks. While surely some of this adaptation was motivated by the missionaries' need to disguise themselves (since the death penalty was meted out to Europeans who entered China illegally [*Letters*, pp. 171-72]), it is also clear that Perboyre wanted to be "all things to all," as he explicitly tells Jacques (*Letters*, p. 145). He insisted that the missionaries should adapt themselves to Chinese customs and spoke his mind when they did not (*Letters*, pp. 203-04). He also worked hard to learn the language; in fact, he felt that he did reasonably well with Chinese. He states that he liked studying it. He found the language rather fascinating, with its tones and its script. "For the Chinese," he wrote, "to read or to recite is to sing" (*Letters*, p. 223).

Perboyre was also convinced of the importance of forming lay Chinese missionaries, judging that they could have a very significant impact among their own people (*Letters*, p. 175). At Houpé he organized dialogue conferences. The methodology was simple. A week ahead of time the subject was announced; e.g., a virtue, or a duty. The following Sunday up to ten lay people preached on that subject. They were young students, catechists, or other "intelligent Christians." At the end, the priest gave some concluding remarks (*Letters*, pp. 255-56).

A typical mission lasted from eight to fifteen days. Missionary life must have been very busy since, not long before his capture, Perboyre tells Monsieur Aladel, the Assistant General in Paris, that he had given seventeen such missions between the feast of the Nativity of the Blessed Virgin Mary and Pentecost. He speaks with great enthusiasm about the first mission in which he preached in Chinese. A native-born confrere, Jean Pe, accompanied him. Perboyre describes Pe with considerable admiration, saying that he bore the burden of the heavy preaching and that he had wonderful pastoral skills (*Letters*, pp. 217-18).

A mission ordinarily proceeded along these lines. When the missionaries arrived in a community they compiled an exact list of all the Christians "adults and children, good and bad" (*Letters*, p. 237). They then had the Christians recite the catechism publicly beginning with the children and proceeding on to the aged. Perboyre notes that the people did this without embarrassment and that parents did not hesitate to allow themselves to be helped, when they faltered, by their children. Then there were baptisms, confessions, first communions, confirmations, marriages, and admission into various confraternities. Generally, the missionaries stayed right in the homes of the people. They ate what the people ate, usually rice (*Letters*, p. 225).

Perboyre remarks that there were sometimes huge numbers of confessions. He declares, in fact, that most Chinese Christians loved to go to confession frequently (*Letters*, p. 282).

He states that the life of the missionaries in China was "completely apostolic" (*Letters*, p. 224), filled with difficulties and dangers. They spent three-quarters of the year roaming from village to village, preaching, catechizing, offering the sacraments, living frugally in a land where most of the Christians themselves were poor (*Letters*, pp. 224-25; cf. p. 175).

Love for the Community

"I would give a thousand lives for it" (Letters, p. 123).

The letters make it clear how attached to the Company Perboyre was. He recalls to his cousin Gabriel how much gratitude they both owe the Congregation for all that it had given them (*Letters*, p. 73).

One of the most frequently recurring themes in his letters is how much God is blessing the little Company. He sees in the goodness of the novices a sign of God's plans for the Company in the future (*Letters*, p. 81; also, pp. 88-89). He is eager to see others become sons of Saint Vincent (*Letters*, p. 23). He is convinced that Saint Vincent continues to attract God's blessings on the Congregation (*Letters*, p. 81).

His letters show warmth toward friends within the Community (cf. *Letters*, pp. 127, 133, 155, 209, 230, 241), as well as a willingness to criticize, in simplicity, what he saw as wrong in the Congregation (*Letters*, p. 269). The latter trait got him into some trouble with his superior, Jean-Baptiste Torrette, who was his classmate from the seminary. John Gabriel takes pains to apologize to Torrette, who had written him a rather sharp letter of rebuke. While Perboyre's letter is apologetic, it also gives little ground. He feels that the missionaries in mainland China were misunderstood and that it would be helpful if both at Macau and in Paris there were someone who had some real experience on the mainland. In this, I suspect, he echoed the sentiments of many a missionary!

Even with these misunderstandings, however, he delights in the unity of the missionaries. He tells his cousin Monsieur Caviole that, though they come from different nations, they work in great harmony, "united by the bonds of the same spirit, at the same time zealous and tireless in carrying on the same works and bearing the same cross" (*Letters*, p. 254).

Devotion to the Blessed Virgin Mary

"The whole world is filled with the mercy of Mary" (Letters, p. 281).

In the letter in which he announces to his uncle the good news of his being sent to China, he adds that his superiors told him his assignment on the Feast of the Purification, which led him to believe that he owed much, in this matter, to the Blessed Virgin (*Letters*, p. 95). In the later years of his life, his love for Mary took on the form of devotion to the Miraculous Medal.

A reading of Perboyre's letters makes it evident that he and others brought the medal to China very soon after the apparitions in Paris and, through it, fostered devotion to Mary.[4] John Gabriel knew Fr. Aladel, Saint Catherine Labouré's spiritual director, quite well. He writes to him in 1838, recounting with enthusiasm the effects that the medal is having in China (*Letters*, p. 281).

Already in 1833, while still in Paris, he had written to his uncle: "The medal of which I have spoken with you is the one that in 1830 was revealed by the Blessed Virgin to a seminarist of the Sisters of Charity" (*Letters*, p. 69). He promises to send his uncle some of the medals, saying that thousands have been distributed in France and in Belgium and that numerous miracles, healings, and conversions have been worked. His letters to his brother Antoine and to his uncle over the following two years make frequent references to the medals and to miracles. He often encloses medals for others to distribute and promises to send them a printed account of the miracles (*Letters*, pp. 76, 79, 83, 85, 89, and 94).

From Jakarta he writes to the Superior General, Fr. Salhorgne, that during a fierce storm that had taken place during their journey, when the waves were like mountains, the missionaries prayed: "O Mary, conceived without sin." He adds that no sooner had they raised their hands toward the Star of the Sea than the tempest subsided (*Letters*, p. 100).

In China he was an eager distributer of the Miraculous Medal (*Letters*, pp. 165, 198). In a letter written shortly before his capture (*Letters*, p. 281) he tells of a young woman who had been brought to him from one of the Christian communities and who had been afflicted by a mental disorder for eight months. The people told him

---

4. When I visited continental China several years ago I was surprised that, almost fifty years after the Communist takeover, so many visible signs of devotion to Our Lady of the Miraculous Medal remained. It is now clear to me, from reading Perboyre, how quickly the medal got there and how rapidly it spread.

that she was anxious to go to confession. Though he doubted the usefulness of hearing her confession, he did so out of compassion. In parting, he gave her a Miraculous Medal. From that day on she began to be healed. Within four or five days she was completely changed.

A Final Thought

It is surely not by chance that these four themes are so prominent in Perboyre's surviving letters. They are all important elements in the tradition that he received as a member of the Vincentian Family and which he handed on to others both as seminary director in France and as a missionary in China. All of the themes are found in the rules (CR II, 3; I, 1 and XI, 10; VIII, 1-2; X, 4) that Saint Vincent gave to his priests and brothers as well as in the contemporary Constitutions of the Vincentians (C 6, 10, 19-25, 49).

Devotion to providence is, at root, belief in the attentive presence of a personal God who walks with us in the dramatically varied experiences of human existence: light and darkness, grace and sin, plan and disruption, peace and turmoil, health and sickness, life and death.

Love for the mission lies at the heart of the Vincentian experience: a deep yearning to follow Christ, evangelizer and servant of the poor, in reaching out effectively to the most abandoned: ministering to them "spiritually and corporally" (SV IX, 59; IX, 593; XI, 364; XI, 592), "in word and in work" (SV XII, 87).

Love for the Community shows itself, basically, in fidelity to our commitments and in our living and working with one another "as friends who love one another deeply" (CR, VIII, 2). One of its clearest expressions is a spirit of thanksgiving for all that God has given us in and through the Company, thus avoiding the perennial temptation to ingratitude, "the crime of crimes," as Saint Vincent calls it (SV III, 37).

Devotion to Mary expresses itself today in a wide variety of ways—the celebration of her feasts, the rosary, the Miraculous Medal—but especially, as Saint Vincent urged, in our being united with her as listeners to the word of God. "Better than anyone else,"

Vincent states, "she penetrated its substance and showed how it should be lived" (SV XII, 129).

If canonizations are for us, then surely these four themes, so striking in the letters of John Gabriel Perboyre, offer us much to reflect on.

Acknowledgements

In one of the chapters of this book I write about how conscious we are, in modern times, of our interdependence. I have sensed that very much in these days. I owe great gratitude to the members of our Vincentian Family, many of whom have encouraged me to publish this work. To be truthful, I have enjoyed writing it. It often came as a welcome diversion in the midst of heavy administrative tasks.

Of course, I get an enormous amount of help. I have ten eyes, arms, and legs here in the secretariat of our General Curia. I want to express my sincerest thanks to Sr. Ann Mary Dougherty (who patiently typed and corrected the manuscript for this book), Sr. Alicia Muñoz, Mrs. Anna Carletti, and Miss Sabrina Mattiuzzo, as well as to Fr. Emeric Amyot d'Inville, the Secretary General, who so ably coordinates the labors of the team. I also deeply appreciate the suggestions and corrections that Frs. Pat Griffin and Tom Davitt have offered me. It is very clear to me that without the assistance of so many people I would have been utterly incapable of bringing this project to completion.